Shadows & Ink

VOL. 1

JOE MYNHARDT

Published by Crystal Lake Publishing
Tales from The Darkest Depths

Website: www.crystallakepub.com

WELCOME
TO ANOTHER

CRYSTAL LAKE PUBLISHING
CREATION

Join today at www.crystallakepub.com & www.patreon.com/CLP

Contents

Introduction

Throughout at least two books, I'll share links to downloadable content, workbooks, exercises, tests, even video lessons and workshops, presented by myself and other industry professionals. Also included, an online forum with everything a horror author might desire, its epicenter a holistic approach to highly-motivated writing, designed to raise your level of creativity and focus.

It's work, but if you find your niche, your voice, and hopefully that balance of fearlessness and inspiration, lightning strikes...and its burn is glorious.

Before you commit to this journey, it is only fair I introduce not only myself, but my qualifications as your guide. My name is Joe Mynhardt, and I've been entrenched in the horror industry for fifteen years. Since 2008 I have worn many hats: writer and editor both fiction and non-fiction, publisher, branding, ad copywriter, and promotional campaign launcher. In 2012 I took the leap and founded Crystal Lake Publishing, and my hands have been stained with the macabre's scarlet ink for over a decade. In 2016 I rolled the dice, quit my day job, and dedicated my life to being a full-time small press publisher. By the time the clock struck 2023, CLP had morphed into Crystal Lake Entertainment, a burgeoning behemoth in the horror domain. We're not just about books anymore. We've branched out into comics, children's literature and activity books, pulp horror, audiobooks, and even representing rights for translations and films. We look for amazing Intellectual Properties and run the full gamut with them.

And if that's not enough, we're on the cusp of venturing into the gaming world.

Since the age of nine, I've devoured books, dissected films, and analyzed plots, so representing Crystal Lake's brand is not a mere job for me. It's a way of life. Publishing and marketing an average of two books a month might sound daunting to most, but not to me. I dedicate an average of 15 hours a day to this endeavor, ensuring that no book is left behind due to the constraints of time. This business isn't just what I do, it's what I breathe. I'm here because I love it, I'm here because I'm a fan. I'm here because I know what it's like when the task of publishing your book or other IP seems insurmountable.

Whether you're a seasoned horror writer or someone looking to bruise your current genre with a dash of horror, I invite you to trust me on this journey. Traversing the terrain of the Shadows & Ink series, the Heartbeat forum, our mastermind group, and the podcast, we'll explore the dark tunnels where secrets lay dormant, the long, eerie nights filled with prowling killers who obey the braying of ravenous wolves...not to mention the slanted house on the hill, the site of so many tragedies.

I promise, it will be a ride to remember.

And it won't hurt.

Okay, maybe a little.

Joe Mynhardt
January, 2024

Section 1: Foundations of Horror & Dark Fiction

Chapter 1
History of Horror Literature

Horror stories have always been a fascinating mirror of our deepest fears and anxieties, painting a vivid picture of the unknown corners of the human mind. These stories range from ancient monster legends hiding in the dark to modern tales exploring the complex workings of the mind. The way horror has evolved shows how much it captivates us. For today's horror writers, going back to the classics isn't just for study—it's like diving into the heart of what makes the genre so gripping.

Let's explore why this trip back in time is so important for the storytellers of today.

- **Understanding the Evolution of Fear:** Delving into classic horror provides a window into the anxieties of past eras. For instance, Mary Shelley's *Frankenstein* grapples with the ethical implications of unchecked scientific ambition during the dawn of the Industrial Revolution, while Bram Stoker's *Dracula* explores the fear of the unknown amidst the backdrop of colonial expansion. By immersing themselves in these tales, writers gain insights into how societal changes shape our darkest fears and how these fears have transformed over time.

- **Appreciating the Mastery of the Craft:** The classics have stood the test of time because of their exceptional storytelling. Giants of the genre, like Edgar Allan Poe and Robert Louis Stevenson, have set benchmarks in creating suspense, developing unforgettable characters, and evoking atmospheric dread. By studying their techniques and narrative structures, modern writers can learn invaluable lessons in the art of storytelling.

- **Finding Inspiration in the Echoes of the Past:** While forging a unique voice is essential, drawing inspiration from the masters can help writers refine their style. The eerie worlds of Lovecraft, the psychological depths explored by Shirley Jackson, or the stark realism of Richard Matheson can serve as guiding beacons. By understanding and resonating with these voices, writers can incorporate elements that enhance their own narratives. You will learn to take the best of them and combine it with your own identity, all in an effort to create something truly unique.

- **Engaging in a Timeless Conversation:** Modern horror often engages in a dialogue with its predecessors, either as a nod of acknowledgment, a reinterpretation, or even as a challenge to established norms. Being well-versed in classic horror allows writers to participate meaningfully in this ongoing conversation, ensuring their contributions are both respectful and innovative.

- **Rekindling the Creative Flame:** Every writer, at some point, faces the daunting abyss of creative block. In such moments, the classics can serve as a beacon, reigniting the spark of inspiration. The moral dilemmas in Stevenson's *Dr Jekyll and Mr Hyde* or the haunting isolation in Henry James' *The Turn of the Screw* can offer fresh perspectives and themes to explore.

- **Balancing Homage with Originality:** A deep understanding of classic horror enables writers to pay tribute to the stories that inspired them. At the same time, this knowledge ensures they avoid unintentional similarities, ensuring their work remains fresh and original.

At their core, classic horror stories are much more than just old tales from the past. They're the foundation the entire genre is built. For modern writers, these stories are like a goldmine filled with wisdom, inspiration, and a connection to the genre's history. As horror stories keep developing, these timeless tales from days gone by help the genre stay true to its rich roots, while also adapting to mirror the constantly changing fears and desires of people.

Ancient and Classical Horror

When we think of horror, our minds might jump to modern tales of haunted houses or eerie ghost stories whispered around campfires. But the roots of horror stretch back much further, to the very dawn of storytelling. From the earliest civilizations, humans have felt the need to explore the unknown, to confront our deepest fears, and to share tales that send shivers down our spines.

One of the earliest known stories, the "Epic of Gilgamesh," isn't just a chronicle of a king's grand adventures. It's a journey into the shadowy realms of the afterlife and the mysteries of existence. Picture a world where the line between gods and mortals was blurred, where eerie encounters weren't just the stuff of legends but a tangible, terrifying reality. The dread of facing such unknowns in a time when myths were lived experiences must have been profound.

But it wasn't just the ancient Mesopotamians who had a flair for the macabre. The Greeks and Romans, with their rich tapestry of myths, introduced us to a whole host of spine-tingling creatures and tales. Imagine the sheer terror of encountering Medusa, her hair a writhing mass of snakes, knowing that one wrong look could turn you to stone (better yet, Medusa was actually being punished). Or the chilling suspense of navigating the labyrinthine corridors of the Minotaur's maze, the beast's roars echoing closer and closer. And it wasn't just myths; the tragedies penned by playwrights like Euripides delved into the darkest recesses of the human soul, exploring themes of madness, betrayal, and the supernatural.

The ancient and classical worlds were rich with stories that resonated with the same fears and anxieties we feel today. They remind us that horror, as a genre, is as old as humanity itself. It's a testament to our enduring fascination with the unknown and our innate need to confront and understand our deepest fears. So, the next time you're curled up with a spine-chilling novel or watching a horror film, remember that you're partaking in a tradition that's been alive for millennia.

Medieval Horror

The medieval era, spanning from the fall of Rome to the dawn of the Renaissance, is a treasure trove for those who relish tales of terror. This period, deeply steeped in religion and societal norms, crafted stories that were as instructive as they were spine-chilling.

The pervasive influence of the church during the Middle Ages cannot be understated. It provided a backdrop of religious fervor, where tales of demons, the devil, and the torments of hell were not just stories...but warnings. Yet, beyond these biblical horrors, the rich folklore of the time brought to life dragons, the undead, and shape-shifters. Whispers of werewolf legends, such as Marie de France's haunting tale of Bisclavret, would dance around the warmth of fires, captivating and cautioning listeners.

Morality tales, too, played a significant role. Works like *The Dance of Death* or "Danse Macabre" served as poignant reminders of mortality, emphasizing that death spared no one, regardless of status. And who could forget Dante's

"Inferno?" This epic journey through the circles of Hell showcased sinners receiving their just desserts in ways that were both terrifying and poetically just.

But the medieval era wasn't just about tales; it was also about the atmosphere. Gargoyles, those stone guardians, sat atop cathedrals not just as architectural wonders but as symbols believed to fend off malevolent forces. The haunted castles of the time, with their shadowy corridors and histories steeped in tragedy, became the stuff of legends and the setting for countless tales of dread.

Visual storytelling also found its place. Manuscripts, akin to today's graphic novels, painted vivid pictures of apocalyptic scenarios. The "Book of Revelation," for instance, showcases harrowing depictions of the end times. Meanwhile, bestiaries, which cataloged both real and mythical creatures, served as both educational tools and sources of nightmarish inspiration.

And let's not forget the chivalric romances. Knights, those paragons of bravery and honor, often found themselves pitted against supernatural foes in dark forests or facing cursed creatures. Their tales were not just about chivalry—they were narratives of confronting the unknown and emerging triumphant.

On a personal note, I will never forget when I read "Beowulf" for the first time. I think I was about nineteen at the time.

The medieval era was a time of rich storytelling, where real-world anxieties melded seamlessly with tales of the supernatural. These narratives, while entertaining, also imparted moral lessons and reflected the hopes, fears, and beliefs of a society in flux.

> We're walking in the footsteps of giants. Every scare we write, every chill we give, owes a little to the horror masters who haunted the pages before u s.

Renaissance to the Enlightenment

The stretch of time from the Renaissance to the Enlightenment was nothing short of transformative. As the world around experienced seismic shifts in art, science, and thought, horror literature also found itself metamorphosing, echoing the era's intricacies.

The Renaissance, often hailed as a period of cultural awakening, breathed new life into classical arts and learning. It was an age where the horizons of knowledge expanded, where the unknown was not just feared but marvellously explored. Yet, as the Enlightenment dawned, the shadows of the macabre still lurked, proving that even in the brightest eras, darkness finds its space.

Gothic influences, with their brooding and towering architectural marvels, persisted, casting long shadows over this age of enlightenment. The Memento Mori, a poignant reminder of life's transience, found its way into both art and tales, urging individuals to remember their mortality amidst the era's advancements.

The supernatural, too, held society in its grip. The fervor of the witch hunts, especially pronounced in the 16th and 17th centuries, saw publications like *The Malleus Maleficarum* offering guidance on identifying and confronting witches. Ghostly tales flourished, painting spirits not just as specters of fear but as tragic souls, yearning for justice and redemption.

Horace Walpole's *The Castle of Otranto* wasn't merely a story; it was a revolution. This pioneering work laid the foundation for the Gothic novel, introducing readers to a world of haunted edifices, unexplained phenomena, and palpable suspense.

But it wasn't just external horrors that captivated writers and readers. The era saw a growing interest in the mysteries of the human mind. Stories delved into themes of duality, with tales of doppelgängers, and explored the unsettling descent into madness, reflecting growing concerns about identity and mental well-being.

The Romantic movement, with its deep reverence for nature, painted the natural world in hues of awe and dread. Nature was no longer just a backdrop; it was a character, mighty and unpredictable. And amidst this movement, Mary Shelley gifted the world *Frankenstein*, a narrative that questioned the very essence of life and the consequences of playing god.

The journey from the Renaissance to the Enlightenment was one of contrasts for horror literature. While the world celebrated reason and discovery, horror tales delved deep, capturing the era's underlying tensions and fears. It was a dance of darkness amidst an age of light, a testament to horror's enduring appeal (don't you just love it?).

19th Century: The Golden Age of Gothic Horror

The 19th century stands out as a golden era for horror literature, a time when the genre truly came into its own. As the world around was in flux, with cities expanding and technology rapidly advancing, there was a palpable tension between the allure of the new and a nostalgia for the old. This juxtaposition—this dance between the past and the present—set the stage for some of the most iconic tales of horror.

Amidst this backdrop of change, writers like Mary Shelley brought to life stories that delved deep into the human psyche. Her *Frankenstein* wasn't merely about a scientist and his monstrous creation. It questioned the very essence of humanity, ambition, and responsibility. Edgar Allan Poe, with his unparalleled ability to tap into the macabre, crafted tales like *The Tell-Tale Heart*, that weren't just spine-chilling but also profound explorations of the mind's darker recesses. Bram Stoker's *Dracula* was more than a vampire tale; it was a reflection on changing societal norms, touching upon themes of sexuality and the clash between old-world traditions and modern aspirations. And then there was Robert Louis Stevenson, whose *Strange Case of Dr Jekyll and Mr Hyde* delved into the duality of human nature, revealing the masks we wear and the shadows lurking within.

The settings of these stories, whether it was a haunting moor or a crumbling castle, weren't just mere backdrops. They breathed life into the narratives, adding layers of atmosphere and evoking a sense of foreboding (we'll cover this in a later chapter). This era also saw a fascinating interplay between the supernatural and the rational. Stories often danced on the edge of reality, teasing the boundaries of what was known and delving into the mysteries of the unknown. And at the heart of many of these tales was a sense of moral ambiguity, where lines between right and wrong, hero and villain, were often blurred, making readers question and ponder long after the last page was turned.

The 19th century was a defining moment for horror literature. The stories from this time, rich in atmosphere and rife with complex themes, have not only shaped the genre but also highlighted the enduring allure of a well-crafted horror tale. They remind us that, at its core, horror is about tapping into our deepest fears, desires, and the timeless questions that haunt the human soul.

Early 20th Century: A New Age of Darkness

The dawn of the 20th century ushered in an age of contrasts. As the world teetered between the remnants of bygone eras and the promise of modernity, horror literature found itself in a unique position to capture the zeitgeist of this boisterous time.

The backdrop of this era was nothing short of dramatic. The world was scarred by the horrors of two World Wars, and the shadows of these conflicts loomed large over literature. At the same time, the rise of psychoanalysis and the march of scientific rationalism began to reshape society's understanding of the self and the universe. These seismic shifts provided a fertile ground for horror tales that mirrored the collective anxieties, hopes, and fears of the age.

Among the luminaries of this period was H.P. Lovecraft, whose tales of cosmic horror introduced readers to a universe both vast and indifferent. His stories, like *The Call of Cthulhu*, didn't just terrify, they challenged our very understanding of humanity's place in the cosmos. M.R. James (a big favorite of mine) with his knack for turning the mundane into the macabre, breathed new life into the ghost story genre, blending academic settings with eerie supernatural twists. And then there was Franz Kafka, whose works, although not strictly horror, delved deep into the existential anxieties of the modern individual, painting a bleak picture of alienation and the often Kafkaesque nature of modern life. If you haven't read his work, I *highly* recommend you do.

The themes that emerged during this period were as varied as they were profound. Lovecraft's cosmic horror reminded us of our insignificance in the face of an uncaring universe. As cities grew and the world became more interconnected, tales began to reflect the isolation and anonymity of urban life, giving birth to a new kind of psychological horror. The rapid pace of technological advancements led writers to question the moral implications of progress, exploring the dark side of innovation. And, of course, the very real horrors of global conflicts found their way into the pages of horror literature, leading to stories that grappled with the depths of human cruelty and the fragility of civilization.

The early 20th century was a transformative period for horror literature. The stories from this time, with their rich tapestry of themes and innovative narrative techniques, not only captured the spirit of the age but also laid the groundwork for future generations of writers. They stand as a testament to the genre's ability to adapt, evolve, and, most importantly, to hold a mirror to society's deepest fears and desires.

Mid to Late 20th Century

The mid to late 20th century was a period of profound transformation, with the world caught in a whirlwind of societal, political, and technological upheavals. As the dust settled from the devastation of World War II and the world grappled with the onset of the Cold War, horror literature found itself in a unique position to capture the collective mood of the times.

This era was a mix of emotions. There was hope because the worst of the war was behind, but also a lot of uncertainty about the future. With new technologies emerging and society changing rapidly, it was both an exciting and nerve-wracking time. And this backdrop was perfect for horror writers to weave their tales.

A standout theme from this period was the deep dive into our minds and societal norms. The world had just seen the extremes of human behavior during the war, and people were trying to process it all. Shirley Jackson was a master at this. She explored the pressures of society and the hidden darkness in stories like *The Lottery* and *The Haunting of Hill House*.

And she wasn't alone. Big names like Stephen King came onto the scene, giving us stories that mirrored the challenges and fears of society, from tales set in small-town America to the haunting corridors of *The Shining*.

But it wasn't just about personal fears. With all the advancements in science and tech, from nuclear power to space journeys, horror stories started asking: "What if we push things too far?" This led to tales about mutants, bleak futures, and the side effects of unchecked progress.

Plus, the big events of the era, like the Cold War tensions and cultural shifts of the '60s and '70s, made their way into horror stories. This added layers of depth, making the narratives more diverse and in tune with the times.

Wrapping it up, the mid to late 20th century was a standout period for horror literature. The stories from this time weren't just scary; they were reflections of society's hopes, fears, and challenges. They set the stage for the horror tales we love today.

Modern era of horror

The modern era is a whirlwind of change, and horror literature has been right there with it, evolving and adapting to the pulse of our times. As we navigate the maze of the digital age, political shifts, and the pressing weight of environmental issues, horror writers have become our guides, crafting stories that echo our shared anxieties and hopes.

One of the most exciting things about today's horror is the chorus of diverse voices singing their unique tales. Think of writers like N.K. Jemisin, Carmen Maria Machado, and Tananarive Due. They're not just telling scary stories. They're challenging us, making us think about race, gender, and who we are in this ever-changing world.

And here's the fun part: modern horror isn't just about ghosts and ghouls anymore. It's playing with sci-fi, dabbling in fantasy, and even borrowing a bit from thrillers. It's like a genre-blending party where tales of tech gone wrong can mingle with stories of cosmic mysteries and deep, introspective journeys. And I love it!

Of course, the world around us plays a big role in shaping these stories. Remember the unsettling times post-9/11? The unease of that era, the feeling of being watched, and the shadows of global threats have all found their way into our tales. And as we grapple with the reality of our planet's future, stories of nature fighting back, or eco-horror, are making waves.

But what truly warms my heart is seeing how inclusive horror has become. It's like a big, spooky tent where everyone's invited. Writers from all walks of life are sharing their nightmares and dreams, ensuring that horror stays fresh, relevant, and oh-so-terrifying.

To wrap it up, modern horror is like a mirror, reflecting our current world with all its wonders and terrors. From the silence of empty cities to the potential dangers of AI, and the ghosts of our pasts, horror keeps us hooked, always ready for another tale to send shivers down our spines. So, buckle up, because the journey through modern horror is a thrilling ride none of us want to miss!

The Future of Horror Literature

Some of the best authors had a way of being ahead of their time. As we know, horror as a genre has always been a reflection of societal anxieties, fears, and the collective unconscious of its time. As we've seen, horror has evolved with the world around it, from the gothic castles of the 19th century to the digital nightmares of the 21st. So, as we stand on the cusp of a new era, marked by rapid technological advancements, socio-political upheavals, and environmental challenges, we can't help but wonder: what's next for horror fiction?

- **Technological Terrors:** The digital age has already made its mark on horror, with stories exploring the dark side of the internet, artificial intelligence, and virtual realities. As technology continues to advance at an unprecedented rate, we can expect horror literature to delve deeper into the implications of these advancements. Themes might include the erosion of privacy, the blending of reality and virtuality, and the potential consequences of AI surpassing human intelligence. Scary stuff!

- **Environmental Horrors:** With climate change becoming an ever more pressing concern, eco-horror is likely to take center stage. Stories might explore post-apocalyptic landscapes, the consequences of bioengineering, and humanity's struggle against nature's wrath. As the real-world implications of environmental neglect become more apparent, horror literature will serve as a cautionary reflection, highlighting the potential horrors that await.

- **Cosmic and Existential Dread:** As our understanding of the universe expands, so too does our realization of our insignificance within it. Modern horror has already begun to explore existential and cosmic dread, and this trend is likely to continue. Stories might delve into the mysteries of the multiverse, the implications of discovering extra-terrestrial life, and the philosophical questions surrounding existence it self.

- **Socio-political Reflections:** The world is in a state of flux, with old societal structures being challenged and new ones emerging. Horror literature will continue to reflect these changes, exploring themes of identity, displacement, and the unknown. As issues of race, gender, and orientation take center stage, horror will offer a platform for diverse voices to share their unique perspectives and fears.

- **Blurring of Genres:** The lines between genres have been blurring for some time now, and this trend is likely to continue. Horror might merge with science fiction, fantasy, and even romance, leading to hybrid genres that offer fresh and innovative narratives. This blending will allow authors to explore new terrains, pushing the boundaries of what horror can be.

- **Interactive and Immersive Horror:** With the rise of virtual reality and augmented reality technologies, the future of horror literature might not be limited to the written word. Readers could find themselves immersed in interactive horror narratives, where they play an active role in the story, navigating haunted houses, interacting with ghosts, or facing their deepest fears in real-time. It's our job as authors to stay up to date with these technologies and adapt.

The future of horror literature is as uncertain as it is exciting. As the world changes, so too will the stories we tell to make sense of it. What remains constant, however, is horror's ability to tap into our deepest fears, offering both a mirror to our anxieties and a cathartic release. Whatever the future holds, one thing is certain: horror will continue to evolve, terrify, and captivate readers for generations to come. And I can't wait.

Chapter 2
Sub-genres of Horror

Horror is a vast and multifaceted genre, with numerous sub-genres that each bring their own flavor of fear to the table. Let's dive into some of the most prominent sub-genres and uncover what makes each one uniquely terrifying:

- Gothic Horror: Distinguished by its moody and atmospheric settings, often in old, decaying mansions or castles. It's less about shock and more about creating a sense of dread and unease. Themes often revolve around decay, madness, and forbidden knowledge. Classics in this sub-genre include Mary Shelley's *Frankenstein*, Edgar Allan Poe's *The Fall of the House of Usher*, and Bram Stoker's *Dracula*.

- Psychological Horror: This sub-genre delves deep into the human psyche, where the horror emerges from emotional instability or distorted perceptions rather than external threats. Shirley Jackson's *The Haunting of Hill House* and Robert Louis Stevenson's *Strange Case of Dr Jekyll and Mr Hyde* are prime examples. Also *The Turn of the* Screw by Henry James. You'll notice that I regularly refer to the same books. I'm sticking with ones I know most people already read. Hopefully.

- Supernatural Horror: Here, the terror arises from encounters with the unknown, be it ghosts, demons, or other supernatural entities.

Noteworthy works include *The Exorcist* by William Peter Blatty and *The Woman in Black* by Susan Hill.

- Cosmic Horror (or Lovecraftian Horror): This sub-genre emphasizes humanity's insignificance in the vast, indifferent cosmos, often featuring ancient and incomprehensible entities. H.P. Lovecraft's tales, such as *The Call of Cthulhu*, *The Shadow over Innsmouth* and *The Dunwich Horror* are quintessential examples.

- Body Horror: A sub-genre that delves into our fears about our own bodies, focusing on grotesque transformations and the fragility of flesh. Clive Barker's *The Books of Blood*, *The Metamorphosis* by Franz Kafka, and films like *The Fly* by David Cronenberg are iconic in this category.

- Splatterpunk: For those who like their horror explicit and gory, splatterpunk offers graphic depictions of violence. Works by Jack Ketchum, John Skipp, Craig Spector, and Richard Laymon exemplify this sub-genre.

- Eco-Horror: Nature strikes back in these tales, which arise from ecological concerns and humanity's impact on the environment. Notable examples include Jeff VanderMeer's *Annihilation*, *The Birds* by Daphne du Maurier, and films like *The Happening* by M. Night Shyamalan.

- Technological Horror: The dark side of technology takes center stage here, exploring everything from malevolent AIs to digital nightmares. Stephen King's *Cell*, *Daemon* by Daniel Suarez, and episodes from the Black Mirror series delve into these themes.

- Slasher: A sub-genre that revolves around a violent antagonist stalking and eliminating victims. While films like *Halloween* and *Scream* are

iconic, novels such as *Psycho* by Robert Bloch, *Final Girls* by Riley
Sager, and *The Last Final Girl* by Stephen Graham Jones also fit the
bill.

- Survival Horror: The emphasis here is on the protagonist's desperate
  fight for survival in hostile settings. Richard Matheson's *I Am Legend*
  and the Resident Evil series are prime examples.

- Erotic Horror: Blending the sensual with the terrifying, this sub-genre
  delves into the darker aspects of desire. Anne Rice's *The Vampire
  Chronicles* and Clive Barker's *Hellbound Heart* are notable works. For
  something a bit more modern, try *Stuck on You* by Jasper Bark.

- Historical Horror: Set against the backdrop of real historical events,
  these tales mix fact with fiction to chilling effect. Dan Simmons' *The
  Terror* and Alma Katsu's *The Hunger* are standout examples.

Horror's many sub-genres offer readers a diverse array of chilling tales, each
reflecting different facets of our deepest fears. As our world and society change,
these sub-genres evolve, ensuring that horror remains a dynamic and ever-rele-
vant form of storytelling. Whether you're drawn to the eerie silences of haunted
mansions or the existential dread of cosmic entities, there's a horror sub-genre
waiting to send shivers down your spine. Too bad we don't have enough time
to read them all.

Navigating the Labyrinth of Horror Sub-genres

In the realm of horror, authors face a crossroads, each path winding into a
different shadowed niche of the genre. The decision to specialize, blend, or
innovate is not just a matter of narrative choice, but a defining element of a
writer's identity.

The Art of Specialization in a Sub-genre:

Choosing to specialize in a sub-genre is akin to mastering a musical instrument. You become attuned to every nuance, every note that can evoke dread. The audience comes to know what to expect: a particular kind of scare, a specific atmosphere. Like a virtuoso, you may become synonymous with the sub-genre itself, your name a byword for a certain kind of darkness.

Yet, there's a shadow to this spotlight. The very expertise that brings readers to your door can become a gilded cage. The expectations of your audience might weigh heavy, and the fear of repetition, of churning out variations on a single theme, can become a specter more haunting than any ghostly tale you pen.

The Fusion Approach: Blending Sub-genres

Then there's the fusion approach, a dance of elements from various horror traditions. It's a creative alchemy that can yield stories with unexpected twists, where a haunted house might also be a spaceship, or a vampire's curse might carry the existential dread of cosmic horror.

This path offers a freedom that specialization does not. Your canvas is broader, your palette richer. But it's not without its pitfalls. The very versatility that allows you to draw from multiple wells can also dilute the potency of your story. And there's the challenge of balance—too much of one element and the delicate harmony of your narrative can tip into discord.

The Path of Innovation: Venturing into New Territories

And what of the trailblazers? Those who step off the map into uncharted territories of terror? Innovation is the lifeblood of the genre, the force that propels it into new eras. To innovate is to invite readers into a world they've never seen, to show them fears they've never felt.

The thrill of this path is undeniable. There's a certain glory in being the first, in knowing that you've added a new chapter to the annals of horror. But the path is fraught with risk. The market may not know what to make of your work, and without the guideposts of genre conventions, the journey can be as daunting as it is exhilarating.

The labyrinth of horror's sub-genres is as intricate and varied as the fears they evoke. Whether an author chooses to become a master of one domain, to mix the elements of many, or to forge ahead into the unknown, their work contributes to the ever-evolving narrative of what scares us. Each choice has its own rewards, its own challenges, and its own place in the grand, dark tapestry of the genre.

In the end, the beauty of horror lies in its adaptability, its capacity to reflect the myriad fears of the human experience. Whether through the focused lens of specialization, the blended brushstrokes of fusion, or the bold colors of innovation, horror continues to captivate and terrify, ensuring its enduring legacy in the pantheon of literature.

> Creativity is a wild mind and a disciplined eye. Let your imagination soar, but guide it with intention.

Originality in Horror

In the world of storytelling, originality is like a lighthouse guiding ships through a stormy sea of familiar tales. For those who weave tales of horror, it's a chance to step off the beaten path and into the shadows of the unknown. But the question that often haunts writers is this: How do you plant the seeds of originality in soil that's been tilled for centuries by countless storytellers before you?

The quest for originality in horror is a journey into the depths of your imagination. It's about peering into the corners of your mind that even you're hesitant to explore. To be original, you must first become an archaeologist of the human psyche, unearthing fears that are personal yet universal, fresh yet fundamentally relatable.

To craft something truly original, you might look where others haven't. It could be a forgotten piece of folklore tucked away in a dusty library book, or a slice of science that's just a little off-kilter. Sometimes, originality lies in the fusion of ideas that seem unrelated—a blending of genres, a clash of concepts, or a character that defies expectations.

Remember, originality doesn't mean ignoring the past. It's about standing on the shoulders of giants and reaching for something they didn't. It's taking the essence of what makes horror so compelling—the fear, the suspense, the surprise—and adding a twist that's all your own. Think of it as a conversation with the greats, where you're both respectful and bold enough to say something new.

Creativity is the soil where the seeds of originality grow. To nurture it, you must give yourself the freedom to think wildly, to dream without limits, and to write without fear of judgment. It's about allowing yourself to make connections that are uniquely yours, to tell stories that only you can tell because they come from a place deep within you.

Originality in horror isn't just about being different for the sake of it. It's about finding a new way to evoke the primal emotions that horror, at its core, is all about. It's a delicate dance between the familiar and the novel, between the expectations of the genre and the surprises you weave into the narrative. As you embark on this journey, remember that the path to originality is as much about the process as it is about the destination.

Let's dive into it even more.

1. Embracing Curiosity: The "What If?" of Horror

Curiosity is the spark that ignites the imagination, and in horror, it's the question "What if?" that often lights the way to originality. This simple, yet profound question can lead writers down paths less trodden, into the dark woods of the unexplored. It's about looking at the world with a sense of wonder and finding inspiration in places that others might overlook. A peculiar news headline, an eerie slice of history, or a personal encounter that sends shivers down the spine—these can all be the seeds of a story that veers from the beaten path.

At its trembling heart, horror pulses with the unknown, the unexplainable, the deeply unsettling. It's a genre that dares to poke at the edges of our understanding, to push us into the shadows where our fears and fascinations intertwine. The "What If?" approach is the key that unlocks these doors, inviting both writer and reader to step through into a world of endless possibilities.

Curiosity is as natural to us as breathing. It's the force that drives us to peel back the layers of the world, to seek out the hidden truths and dare to ask the questions that might otherwise go unspoken. In horror, this curiosity is a blade that cuts both ways—drawing us in with the promise of answers, yet often leading us to confront horrors we might wish remained hidden.

When we ask "What if?" we're doing more than just speculating—we're crafting the foundation of a horror story. "What if there was a curse tied to a videotape?" "What if a house was a gateway for malevolent spirits?" "What if the line between life and death could be blurred?" These questions are the seeds from which the twisted trees of horror grow, each branch a narrative possibility.

The true power of the "What If?" lies in its embrace of the possible. Horror stories that flirt with the edges of reality, that suggest their terrifying events could happen, resonate with a chilling authenticity. They blur the line between fiction and reality, making the reader's heartbeat quicken with the thought, "This could happen to me."

Moreover, this approach is an invitation to the imagination. It asks both the writer and the reader to ponder the consequences of the hypothetical, to explore the limits of their fears, and to engage in a silent dialogue with the unfolding story.

To embrace curiosity and the "What If?" in horror is to celebrate our intrinsic need to explore and question. It's an acknowledgment of that fine line between the known and the unknown and the courage to step over it. Horror, like life, is an expedition into the uncharted, propelled by the relentless flame of curiosity. It's this thrilling expedition, with all its shadows and revelations, that keeps the heart of horror beating and its readers endlessly enthralled.

One of my first tales to make it to print sprang from a rather unnerving realization—I was parked in a spot notorious for carjackings, and "What If" worked itself into my mind. The fear that crept up on me, mingled with a surge of anger, became the fuel for my writing. I channeled those raw emotions into a story that stood apart from the rest. And how could I be so sure it was different? Well, I'm an avid reader. I've devoured countless stories, so I have a pretty good grasp on what's been done to death and what hasn't. That knowledge is a powerful tool; it helps me carve out spaces for my own stories in the vast library of literature.

We are of course born with this intrinsic need to explore and question, but some of us lose it along the way. Childhood is often remembered as a time of boundless curiosity, a period when the world seemed vast, mysterious, and filled with endless possibilities. Every shadow held a story, every rustle of leaves whispered secrets, and every new experience was an adventure waiting to be embarked upon. As we grow older, the weight of responsibilities, societal expectations, and the routine of daily life can sometimes dim this innate sense of wonder. However, reflecting back on our childhood curiosity can offer invaluable insights, rekindling our passion for exploration and reigniting the flames of imagination.

Children view the world with an unfiltered lens, free from the biases and pre-conceptions that often cloud adult perception. For a child, every day presents a myriad of questions:

"Why is the sky blue?"

"How do birds fly?"

"Where do dreams come from?"

This relentless quest for knowledge stems from a genuine desire to understand the world around them. It's a reminder of a time when we weren't afraid to ask questions, no matter how naive or trivial they might seem.

For children, the joy lies not just in finding answers but in the process of discovery itself. The world is a treasure trove of mysteries, and every revelation, whether it's the discovery of a hidden nook in the garden or the realization that rainbows appear after the rain, is celebrated with genuine delight. This sense of wonder, of finding magic in the mundane, is something that often gets lost in the transition to adulthood. Yet, it's a perspective that can add richness and depth to our experiences, transforming the ordinary into the extraordinary. I'm convinced that this vibrant spark of curiosity is what makes authors, particularly those who dabble in the macabre, resonate so harmoniously at conventions and book signings. They exude an infectious energy, a zest for the curious and the thrilling... a sense of adventure. And, of course, there's always a hint of mischief twinkling in their eyes. It's why fans want to buy them drinks.

Reflecting on our childhood curiosity is not just an exercise in nostalgia. It's an invitation to reconnect with our inner child. It challenges us to break free from the shackles of routine, to look at the world with fresh eyes, and to embrace the unknown with open arms. Whether it's picking up a new hobby, traveling to an unfamiliar destination, or simply taking a moment to observe the world around us, there are countless ways to rekindle our sense of wonder.

Embracing our childhood curiosity in adulthood can have profound benefits. It fosters creativity, encouraging us to think outside the box and approach problems from different angles. It promotes lifelong learning, reminding us that there's always something new to discover, no matter our age. Most importantly, it enriches our lives, adding a layer of depth and meaning to our experiences.

Childhood curiosity is a precious gift, a beacon that guides us through the complexities of life. By reflecting on this innate sense of wonder, we can navigate the challenges of adulthood with grace, resilience, and a zest for life. In the end, curiosity is not just about seeking answers; it's about celebrating the journey, cherishing the moments of discovery, and reveling in the magic of the unknown. Perhaps this is the secret to a happy life. To the fountain of youth.

2. Cross-pollination of Genres:

One way to infuse originality into horror is by drawing inspiration from other genres. A horror story with the intricate plotting of a mystery, the world-building of science fiction, or the emotional depth of a romance can result in a narrative that feels fresh and unexpected. By blending elements from diverse genres, authors can create a unique tapestry of horror that defies categorization. Consider the film *Rocky* with Sylvester Stallone. While it may seem like a sports movie on the surface, at its heart, it's truly a tale of romance.

3. Cultural Exploration:

Horror is a universal emotion, but its manifestations vary across cultures. By exploring myths, legends, and folklore from different parts of the world, authors can introduce readers to unfamiliar terrors. This not only enriches the narrative with diverse perspectives but also offers a fresh take on what scares us.

Horror, as a genre, has always been a reflection of society's deepest fears and anxieties. While many of these fears are universal, their manifestations and interpretations can vary widely across cultures. Cultural exploration in horror literature provides a unique lens through which readers can experience the unfamiliar, broadening their understanding of the world and the myriad ways in which horror can be expressed.

Cultural exploration in horror delves into the myths, legends, and folklore of different societies, offering readers a glimpse into the unique terrors that haunt different corners of the world. This not only enriches the narrative with diverse perspectives but also challenges readers to confront their own biases and preconceptions. By immersing themselves in a different cultural context, readers are forced to re-evaluate their understanding of horror, recognizing that what might be terrifying in one culture might be benign or even revered in another.

Notable Examples in Horror Literature:

- *The Ballad of Black Tom* by Victor LaValle: This novella reimagines H.P. Lovecraft's "The Horror at Red Hook", addressing the original's racial prejudices. Set in 1920s Harlem, LaValle's story offers a fresh perspective on Lovecraftian horror, exploring themes of racism and cultural alienation in America.

- *Ring* by Koji Suzuki: This Japanese horror novel, which inspired the famous film adaptations, delves into the urban legends and technological anxieties of modern Japan. The story of a cursed videotape draws from Japanese folklore, presenting a unique blend of traditional and contemporary fears.

- *The Fisherman* by John Langan: While not set in a non-Western culture, Langan's novel is a masterclass in world-building, creating a richly detailed mythology rooted in the history and geography of upstate New York. The narrative weaves together various cultural and historical threads, crafting a tapestry of horror that feels both ancient and modern.

- *Mexican Gothic* by Silvia Moreno-Garcia: Set in 1950s Mexico, this novel draws on Mexican history and folklore to craft a chilling tale of haunted houses and family secrets. The story challenges Western Gothic conventions, infusing them with a distinctly Mexican sensibility.

- *The Devourers* by Indra Das: This novel offers a fresh take on werewolf legends, set against the backdrop of India's rich history and diverse cultures. Das weaves together narratives from the Mughal era and contemporary Kolkata, exploring themes of identity, colonialism, and transformation.

Cultural exploration in horror literature serves a dual purpose. On one hand, it introduces readers to the rich tapestry of global horror traditions, expanding their horizons and deepening their appreciation for the genre. On the other hand, it challenges authors to think beyond the familiar, to seek inspiration in the stories, myths, and legends of cultures different from their own.

Moreover, in an increasingly globalized world, cultural exploration in literature promotes understanding and empathy. It underscores the idea that while the specifics of our fears might differ, the emotion itself is universal. Horror, in all its culturally diverse manifestations, reminds us of our shared humanity.

4. Challenging Conventions:

Innovation in horror writing often requires a bold step away from the comfort of well-worn paths. Authors who aspire to bring something new to the table must be ready to confront and challenge the established norms that have long defined the genre. This is no small feat, though. It involves a deliberate effort to subvert expectations and breathe fresh life into familiar tropes.

One way to challenge conventions is by flipping them on their head. Consider the trope of the final girl in slasher films and stories—the sole survivor who outlives her companions. An innovative approach might present her not as a victim of circumstance but as the mastermind behind the events, or perhaps explore the story from the perspective of the antagonist, offering a narrative that sympathizes with the 'monster.'

Playing with narrative structure can also serve as a powerful tool for innovation. Non-linear storytelling, unreliable narrators, or mixed media formats within the text can disorient and re-engage the reader, providing a new experience of suspense and discovery. For example, a story might be told through a series of diary entries, police reports, and online forum threads, requiring the reader to piece together the truth. I'm certain you're familiar with *Carrie* by Stephen King or *World War Z* by Max Brooks. A newer example is one of our very own anthologies, *Dead Letters*, edited by Jacob Steven Mohr.

Reimagining classic monsters in a contemporary context is another avenue for challenging conventions. What would creatures like vampires, werewolves, or ghosts represent in today's world? Authors might place these entities in unexpected settings—such as a corporate office or a post-apocalyptic landscape—exploring themes relevant to modern society, like the fear of technology or the breakdown of social order.

By pushing these boundaries, authors not only contribute to the evolution of the genre but also invite readers to question and rethink their own preconceptions about horror. This can lead to a more engaged and critical readership, eager for stories that offer more than just scares. Stories that provoke thought, challenge societal norms, and offer commentary on the human condition.

In doing so, authors can redefine what horror means for a new generation. They can transform the genre into a vessel for exploring the complexities of contemporary life, all while delivering the thrills and chills that horror aficionados crave. It's through this delicate balance of respect for tradition and the courage to innovate that the future classics of horror literature are born.

5. Personal Reflection:

The quest for originality in horror often leads writers to the most intimate and shadowed corners of their own minds. It's within these personal recesses that the most compelling and relatable fears dwell. When authors dare to mine the depths of their own experiences, they tap into a wellspring of authenticity that can transform the written word into a mirror reflecting the human condition.

Personal reflection in writing is not merely about recounting events but about connecting with the emotional truths that underlie those experiences. An author might draw upon the vulnerability felt during a childhood illness, the isolation of being misunderstood, or the heart-pounding rush of a close escape. These emotions, when woven into the fabric of a narrative, create a tapestry of horror that is both unique and universally relatable.

The power of personal reflection lies in its ability to evoke empathy. Readers may not have lived the exact circumstances presented in the story, but the emotional landscape is familiar territory. The fear of loss, the dread of the unknown, the sting of betrayal—these are sentiments that resonate with a wide audience. By grounding horror in the personal, authors give voice to the silent screams and whispered worries that we all harbor.

Moreover, writing from a place of personal reflection can lead to narratives that challenge the reader's own perceptions and biases. It invites them to confront not just the monsters on the page but also the ones that lurk in the recesses of their own psyche. This introspective journey can be both unsettling and cathartic, as it often shines a light on universal truths about fear, courage, and the human spirit.

In essence, personal reflection in horror writing is a conduit for exploring the shared anxieties of our collective experience. It's a brave act of vulnerability that, when executed with sincerity, can yield stories that linger in the consciousness long after the final page is turned. These are the stories that don't just scare us, but also connect us, reminding us that we are not alone in our fears, and in that connection lies the true power of horror. Perhaps this is precisely why we love the genre so much.

6. Continuous Learning:

While this topic might seem like a natural fit for the Writer's Life section of the book, I believe it's essential to address it in this part of our discussion. The relentless march of time ensures that the world we live in is never static. It's a dynamic, ever-evolving tapestry of events, discoveries, and revolutions that shape the human experience. For the horror writer, this constant change is not just background noise. It's a fertile ground for inspiration, a veritable feast of ideas ripe for the picking.

Staying abreast of the times means tuning into the pulse of the present—it's about understanding the latest scientific breakthroughs, the societal shifts that unsettle us, and the technological advancements that promise to reshape our reality. Consider the rapid development of artificial intelligence: it's not just a technological marvel but a wellspring of existential questions. What does it mean to be human in an age where machines can think, learn, and perhaps even feel? This innovation stirs a spectrum of reactions, with people often responding in polar opposites—some with awe at the potential for progress and others with deep-seated fear of the unknown implications. These divergent views on AI underscore the profound impact it has on our collective psyche, challenging our preconceptions and forcing us to confront the future we are rapidly hurtling toward.

Then there's the vast expanse of space, a frontier that has always captivated the human imagination. As we probe deeper into the cosmos, we uncover mysteries that dwarf our earthly concerns. The horror writer can harness this cosmic scale to evoke a sense of awe and terror—the fear of the vast, indifferent universe is a potent source of dread.

On our own planet, the specter of climate change looms large. It's a slow-motion disaster that's all too real, providing a backdrop for stories that explore the consequences of humanity's actions. The horror in these narratives is not just in the monstrous storms or the rising seas but in the realization of our own vulnerability and the fragility of the civilizations we've built.

By engaging with the world's changes, authors can craft stories that resonate with the zeitgeist. These tales become more than just entertainment—they're reflections of our collective anxieties and aspirations. They challenge readers to confront the uncomfortable questions of our time and consider the implications of the paths we're currently walking.

Understand that the evolving world is a canvas for the horror writer, an invitation to explore the unknowns of our era and to imagine the possibilities that lie just beyond the horizon. It's a call to weave the threads of change into narratives that thrill, challenge, and terrify. As the world changes, so too does the nature of our fears, and it is the horror writer's privilege to chronicle these fears for a world that is eager to read, reflect, and perhaps even be changed by them.

In later volumes of this series, we'll dive deeper into continuous learning and look at some examples as well as workshops worthy of your time.

Why is it crucial for authors and publishers to update their knowledge and skills about AI?

- Staying Relevant: As AI and automation become more prevalent, many traditional jobs are at risk. Continuous learning ensures that individuals remain valuable and irreplaceable in the job market. Reflecting on my own career, the transformation over the last decade has been immense. It's a significant investment of time, but staying current is an integral part of my job. Consider the advent of the internet—businesses that failed to adapt quickly found themselves left behind. And make no mistake, your career as an author is very much a business. Just as those early digital pioneers had to evolve or face obsolescence, we as writers must continually adapt to the changing landscape of publishing and reader engagement to ensure our work remains relevant and our careers viable.

- Ethical Implications: Understanding AI is not just about leveraging its benefits but also about recognizing its ethical implications. Issues like data privacy, algorithmic bias, and the societal impact of automation require informed discussions and decisions.

- Informed Decision Making: For businesses, staying updated on the latest AI technologies can lead to better decision-making, improved operational efficiency, and a competitive edge in the market.

In the age of AI, continuous learning is the key to navigating the challenges and opportunities of the future. Whether it's mastering a new programming language, understanding the nuances of machine learning, or exploring the ethical dimensions of AI, a commitment to lifelong learning will empower individuals to thrive in an increasingly AI-driven world.

AI, at its core, is about creating machines that can think and act intelligently. This encompasses a wide range of applications, from machine learning algorithms that can predict consumer behavior to natural language processing systems that can understand and generate human-like text. The potential of AI is vast, and its impact is felt across sectors, from healthcare and finance to entertainment and education.

Let's look at some examples of New Tech Influenced by AI:

- Autonomous Vehicles: Self-driving cars, once a staple of science fiction, are now becoming a reality. Companies like Tesla, Waymo, and Uber are investing heavily in AI systems that can navigate complex urban environments, make split-second decisions, and ensure passenger safety.

- Healthcare Diagnostics: AI-powered tools like IBM's Watson can analyze vast amounts of medical data in seconds, assisting doctors in diagnosing diseases, predicting patient outcomes, and personalizing treatment plans.

- Virtual Assistants: Siri, Alexa, and Google Assistant are AI-driven virtual assistants that have become integral parts of many people's daily lives. They can answer questions, control smart home devices, play music, and even make reservations.

- Chatbots: Many businesses now use AI-powered chatbots for customer service. These chatbots can handle a wide range of queries, schedule appointments, and even process orders, offering a seamless customer experience.

- Deepfake Technology: Using AI, it's now possible to create hyper-realistic but entirely fake content. Deepfakes can generate convincing videos of real people saying or doing things they never did, raising concerns about misinformation and digital trust.

- Predictive Analytics: Companies like Netflix and Amazon use AI to analyze user behavior and preferences, predicting what movies a user might enjoy or what products they might want to purchase next.

By staying in touch with these developments we are not only more connected to the world around us, but we'll be able to be a part of those important conversations about AI, and if nothing else, this journey will serve as a wellspring of inspiration, providing even more ideas for captivating stories that beckon to be told.

To finish, originality in horror is not about reinventing the wheel but about viewing the familiar through a fresh lens. It requires a blend of curiosity, courage, and introspection. For authors willing to venture into uncharted territories, the rewards are manifold: the thrill of discovery, the joy of connecting with readers in new ways, and the satisfaction of contributing to the rich legacy of horror literature.

Writing is not always about the light at the end of the tunnel, but finding your way through the dark.

Chapter 3

Key elements and tropes in horror fiction

When we talk about the "key elements" in the realm of horror and dark fiction, we're diving into the essential ingredients that make these stories so spine-chillingly good. These are the nuts and bolts that hold together the framework of a story that's meant to scare, unsettle, and keep you up at night. Think of them as the secret spices in a recipe that make a dish unforgettable. In horror and dark fiction, these elements are the narrative twists, the thematic shadows, and the stylistic choices that writers use to craft tales that linger in your mind long after you've turned the last page. Let's unpack these a bit and see what makes the genre tick. We'll dive into each one a bit more later on.

In the shadowy corners of horror and dark fiction, the **atmosphere** is everything. It's the canvas where the story paints its chills and thrills. Picture the classic haunted house, its corridors shrouded in cobwebs, or the eerie silence of a fog-laden forest. It's not just about a place that looks scary; it's about creating a mood that crawls under your skin and whispers of danger at every turn. This atmosphere of dread and foreboding is the heartbeat of horror, setting the stage for a tale that's as much about the vibe as it is about the plot.

Then there's the **fear of the unknown**, that primal instinct that tells you to be wary of what you can't understand or see. Horror thrives on this fear, serving up a buffet of supernatural entities and mind-bending phenomena that defy explanation. It's the shadow that moves just out of the corner of your eye or the voice that whispers your name when you're certain you're alone. This fear keeps us riveted, turning page after page in search of answers we're not sure we want.

Suspense is the art of the tease in horror storytelling. It's the slow build, the tightening of tension that makes your palms sweat and your heart race. Like a maestro conducting an orchestra, a good horror story knows just when to hold back and when to unleash the terror. It's the anticipation of the scare that often holds more power than the scare itself, the waiting for the other shoe to drop that keeps us hooked.

Isolation in horror is a potent tool, but it's a delicate dance between solitude and interaction. It's about stripping away the safety net, leaving characters to face their fears without the comfort of company. Imagine the terror of being the only one left in a town where shadows move with sinister intent, or the suffocating silence of a space station where the only sound is your own breathing. This solitude amplifies the horror, making every decision, every step, fraught with tension.

However, it's crucial to balance this isolation with moments of connection. A story needs the spark of interaction to drive the drama forward. Without another soul for the protagonist to clash with, to confide in, or to question, the narrative risks losing its dynamic edge. The antagonist, too, requires a counterpart to reveal their full menace and motive. It's in the interplay between characters that the drama unfolds, the tension rises, and the horror becomes a shared experience that resonates with the reader. So while isolation can be a storyteller's ally, it must not overshadow the need for compelling character interactions that are the lifeblood of any good story.

Supernatural elements are the bread and butter of many horror tales. Ghosts that rattle chains, demons that bargain for souls, and witches that cackle over cauldrons—these are the beings that populate our nightmares, representing the inexplicable and uncontrollable forces that we can neither predict nor understand.

Psychological horror, on the other hand, turns the lens inward, exploring the abyss that is the human mind. It's not about what's lurking in the closet, but what's lurking in the recesses of our psyche—our fears, our madness, our darkest desires. This sub-genre makes us question not just the reality of the characters, but our own sanity as well.

Beneath the surface of many horror stories lie deep **moral and philosophical questions**. These tales force us to confront the nature of good and evil, to ponder the consequences of our actions, and to examine the societal norms we take for granted. Horror often holds up a mirror to humanity, asking us to look closely at what we see reflected there.

The power of **unsettling imagery** in horror cannot be overstated. It's the graphic description that makes you wince, the vivid scene that plays on loop in your mind's eye long after you've finished the story. This imagery is crafted to disturb, to unsettle, to leave a lingering sense of unease that's hard to shake.

Twists and revelations are the jolts of electricity that keep a horror story buzzing. They're the moments that make you gasp, the turns that flip your understanding upside down. A well-placed twist can transform the entire narrative, making you question everything you thought you knew about the story.

Lastly, **vulnerability** is the thread that ties all these elements together. It's what makes the characters relatable and the horror personal. Whether it's the terror of being chased by something monstrous or the haunting weight of past guilt, vulnerability is what makes the stakes feel real. It's the reminder that in horror, just like in life, we're all just one step away from the edge.

These key elements work in tandem to create the unique emotional response that horror and dark fiction aim to evoke in readers. They are the tools that writers use to craft tales that chill, thrill, and linger long after the final page is turned.

Which brings us to tropes.

Diving into the world of horror, we find ourselves surrounded by tropes—those recurring motifs that make the genre so delightfully shiver-inducing. Tropes are the seasoning in the stew of storytelling, providing that familiar taste that keeps us coming back for more. But it's not just about throwing in a pinch of this or a dash of that; it's about how these ingredients blend together to create something unexpected and new.

Let's take a closer look at some of these classic horror tropes and see how they can be used to stir up some truly spine-tingling tales:

- The Haunted House: More than just creaky floorboards and chilling drafts, the haunted house trope plays on our deepest fears of the unknown lurking in our own homes. It's the history soaked into the walls, the whispers of past tragedies that echo through the halls, that make these stories so compelling. But the real trick is to turn the familiar on its head, to make the safety of 'home' the most dangerous place of all. Recommended reading: Shirley Jackson's *The Haunting of Hill House*.

- The Final Girl: She's the one we root for, the survivor, the unexpected warrior. Often, she starts as the underdog, but her journey is one of transformation. The Final Girl trope isn't just about survival; it's a commentary on resilience and the subversion of expectations. To keep her fresh, writers can give her depth and flaws, making her victory all the more satisfying. Not a book, but Laurie Strode from John Carpenter's Halloween series will always be the best example.

- The Vengeful Ghost: This trope taps into our sense of justice and the fear that wrongs will come back to haunt us—quite literally. The key to a memorable vengeful ghost story is in the backstory; the more tragic or unjust, the more we're invested in the ghost's quest for closure. Recommended reading: *The Woman in Black* by Susan Hill.

- The Forbidden Ritual: There's something inherently human about the desire to touch the untouchable, to know the unknowable. The forbidden ritual trope is a dance with danger, a flirtation with the ultimate consequences. The thrill for the reader is in the anticipation, the knowledge that some lines should never be crossed. Recommended reading: *The Ritual* by Adam Nevill.

- The Innocent Bystander: Thrown into chaos, the innocent bystander is our stand-in, the everyman or everywoman who reacts as we might in the face of horror. Their normalcy is the contrast that amplifies the abnormal, and their journey is a tightrope walk between the mundane and the monstrous. Recommended reading: *Cell* by Stephen King.

- The Creepy Child: Children represent innocence, but when that innocence is twisted, the effect is deeply unsettling. The creepy child trope works because it inverts our expectations. To keep this trope fresh, writers can explore the 'why'—the reasons behind the child's behavior that are as complex as they are horrifying. Recommended reading: *The Exorcist* by William Peter Blatty.

- The Unbeliever: Skepticism is healthy, but in horror, the unbeliever's denial can be a death sentence. This trope serves as a cautionary tale about the dangers of closed-mindedness. The challenge is to make the unbeliever's arc believable and to use their skepticism as a tool that adds tension and conflict. Recommended reading: *Heart-Shaped Box* by Joe Hill.

- The Twist Ending: We all love a good surprise, especially when it makes us question everything we've read so far. The twist ending is a staple of horror that, when done well, can elevate a story from good to unforgettable. The secret is to lay the groundwork so that the twist feels earned, not cheap. Recommended reading: *I Am Legend* by Richard Matheson.

- The Cabin in the Woods: Isolation is terrifying, and the cabin in the woods is the epitome of being cut off from the world. It's the perfect setting for horror to unfold, away from prying eyes and helping hands. But the real twist comes when the isolation outside is mirrored by the isolation between characters, ramping up the tension. Recommended reading: *Cabin at the end of the World* by Paul Tremblay.

- The Eldritch Tome: Books hold knowledge, and in horror, knowledge can be deadly. The eldritch tome trope is about the thirst for knowledge—and the price paid for quenching it. The allure is in the forbidden, in the idea that some things are beyond human comprehension for a reason. Recommended reading: *The King in Yellow* by Robert W. Chambers.

- The Cursed Object: It's the seemingly mundane that becomes a vessel for terror. The cursed object trope plays on our fear of the ordinary turned sinister. The twist? It's not just about the object's curse, but its history, its journey through hands innocent and guilty, and the web of lives it tangles along the way. Recommended reading: *Christine* by Stephen King.

- The Ominous Warning: The ignored prophecy, the dismissed advice of the wise—this trope is a dance with destiny. It's not just about the warning itself, but the weight of fate it carries. The key is to weave the warning into the fabric of the story, making it a puzzle piece the reader and characters fail to place until it's too late. Recommended reading: Edgar Allan Poe's "The Masque of the Red Death."

- The Mirror Scare: Mirrors are gateways, reflections of our true selves, or, in horror, something much more sinister. The mirror scare trope is effective because it confronts us with the unexpected in the familiar. To refresh this trope, the reflection could reveal not just a scare, but a truth, a secret that shatters as profoundly as the glass. Recommended reading: *The Broken Girls* by Simone St. James.

- The Sleepwalker: The vulnerability of our unconscious selves gives the sleepwalker trope its edge. It's the horror of not knowing what you're capable of when you're not in control. The innovation here can come from intertwining the dream world with reality, blurring the lines until neither the character nor the reader can tell them apart. Recommended reading: *Sleepwalker* by Karen Robards.

- The Doppelgänger: Our doubles, our shadows, our 'what ifs.' The doppelgänger trope is a confrontation with the self—the person we could have been. The fresh take? It's not just about the evil twin, but the choices that lead us down different paths, the doppelgänger as a dark mirror of possibility. Recommended reading: *The Outsider* by Stephen King (yes, I'm a huge King fan).

- The Sinister Town: The trope of the sinister town is a canvas for societal fears, a microcosm of a world gone wrong. To reinvent this trope, the town becomes a character, its dark secrets woven into its very foundations, and its inhabitants unknowingly part of a larger, more terrifying story. Recommended reading: *Salem's Lot* by Stephen King.

- The Unkillable Monster: The monster that won't die is the embodiment of our fears of death and the unknown. To breathe new life into this trope, the focus shifts to the 'why'—the reason behind the monster's invincibility, perhaps a curse, a mistake, or a tragedy that refuses to be forgotten. Recommended reading: *It* by Stephen King.

- The Buried Secret: What's more horrifying than a secret? A secret that refuses to stay buried. This trope thrives on the past's grip on the present. The innovation comes in the layers of the secret, a mystery that, when unraveled, reveals more than just the horror at its core, but the human heart as well. Recommended reading: *The Secret History* by Donna Tartt.

- The Possession: The loss of self, the invasion of the soul—the possession trope is horror at its most intimate. The new angle? The entity's perspective, its history, its desires, and fears, making the possession a tragic tale of two beings caught in a struggle for existence. Recommended reading: *The Exorcist's House* by Nick Roberts.

- The Mad Scientist: The archetype of the mad scientist, driven by hubris and curiosity, taps into our fear of unchecked ambition and science gone awry. To refresh this trope, consider the scientist's humanity, their backstory, and the ethical dilemmas that push them over the edge. What if their madness is not just in the mind, but a contagion that can spread? Recommended reading: *Frankenstein* by Mary Shelley.

- The Clown or Doll: Objects of innocence turned malevolent, clowns and dolls are effective because they subvert comfort and familiarity. To innovate, these figures could be vessels for more than just evil—they might hold memories, embody lost innocence, or be the last remnants of love turned into a twisted mockery. Recommended reading: *String Them Up* by William Sterling.

- The Forbidden Room: The lure of the forbidden room is the temptation of the taboo, the secret we are not meant to uncover. In reimagining this trope, the room itself could be a sentient entity, or perhaps it's not the room that's forbidden, but the memories or truths it contains, which are part of a much larger, cosmic puzzle. Recommended reading: *The Yellow Wallpaper* by Charlotte Perkins Gilman.

- The Urban Legend: Urban legends are the modern folklore, the stories we tell to make sense of the unexplainable in our contemporary world. To give this trope a new spin, the legend could be a misdirection, a cover-up for something far more real and sinister, or perhaps it's a collective belief that brings the horror into existence. Recommended reading: *The Vanishing Hitchhiker: American Urban Legends and Their Meanings* by Jan Harold Brunvand.

- The Disbelieving Authorities: The trope of disbelieving authorities represents our frustration with those who refuse to see the truth. To subvert this, what if the authorities are all too aware of the horror, but their disbelief is a facade to protect a darker secret of their own? Recommended reading: *Dracula* by Bram Stoker.

- The Unexpected Savior: The trope of the unexpected savior speaks to the potential within us all to rise to greatness. To deepen this trope, the savior's journey could be one of self-discovery, where the horror they face is intricately tied to their own transformation and the realization of their hidden strength. Recommended reading: *The Stand* by Stephen King.

- The Bloody Message: A message written in blood is a visceral image of terror. To expand upon this, the message could be part of an ancient language or code, a puzzle that, once solved, reveals not just a warning, but a prophecy or a call to action that is central to the character's fate.

Red Dragon by Thomas Harris.

- The Mysterious Stranger: The mysterious stranger is a harbinger of change, often bringing knowledge or warning. To refresh this trope, the stranger could be a time traveler, a being from another dimension, or even an aspect of the protagonist themselves, challenging the very fabric of reality. *Something Wicked This Way Comes* by Ray Bradbury.

- The Resurrection: The resurrection trope plays on our fear of death and the unnatural return to life. To reinvent this, the resurrected could come back wrong, not just in body, but in time and place, creating ripples that alter the course of history or reality itself. Recommended reading: *Pet Cemetary* by Stephen King.

These tropes, when handled with originality and care, can become more than just familiar beats in a horror story—they can be the keys to unlocking new nightmares, the sparks that ignite a fresh inferno of fear. They are the signposts in the fog, guiding us into the heart of darkness. For the horror writer, these tropes are not just clichés to be trotted out but challenges to be met, opportunities to turn the expected on its head and to craft tales that linger long after the last page is turned, like a shadow that persists even when the light is gone.

When you write, you create more than just stories; you build bridges to your readers' hearts and minds.

Techniques to master

Red Herrings:

Red Herrings in horror fiction are like the creaky floorboards in an old house—they're there to make you jump, to look the wrong way, while the real scare sneaks up from behind. These clever little distractions are the author's way of keeping you on your toes, guessing at shadows while the true monster lurks just out of sight.

Let's chat about these mischievous plot devices, shall we? Picture this: you're deep into a horror novel, the kind that has you checking the locks twice before bed. You've got this hunch about who the ghost haunting the protagonist is. But then, out of nowhere, a character who seemed as harmless as a basket of kittens starts acting suspicious. You're now convinced they're behind it all. That's a red herring for you—a clue or a character thrown into the story to lead you astray.

Take the classic *And Then There Were None* by Agatha Christie. Not strictly horror, but bear with me. The isolated setting, the mounting tension, the creeping dread as characters are picked off one by one—it's got all the trappings of a horror story. Christie was a master of the red herring, scattering them like breadcrumbs for readers to follow, only to lead them in circles.

Or how about *The Turn of the Screw* by Henry James? This tale is a veritable dance of red herrings, with its ambiguous ghosts and the unreliable narration that has you questioning what's real and what's not. It's like trying to follow a map in the dark; just when you think you know where you're going, you run into a wall.

Modern horror loves to play this game, too. In *The Girl With All the Gifts* by M.R. Carey, we're led to believe that the story is about one thing—a dystopian world overrun by 'hungries,' but as the layers peel back, we find it's about so much more. The red herrings in this tale are not just plot twists but also challenge our perceptions of humanity and morality.

And let's not forget the slasher genre, where red herrings are practically part of the dress code. Take Friday the 13th—the films, sure, but the novelization by Simon Hawke, as well. You spend so much time suspecting the wrong camp counselor, the tension building with each turned page, only to find out the killer's identity is far more shocking.

So, why do horror authors love to sprinkle their stories with red herrings? It's simple: they make the story unpredictable. They keep the pages turning and the lights on. They're the secret ingredient in the recipe for a tale that sticks with you, the kind that has you jumping at the sound of the wind against your window.

In the end, red herrings are not just about misdirection. They're about engagement, about drawing the reader into an active dialogue with the story. They invite you to be a detective, to question everything, and to embrace the thrill of the unknown. And isn't that what horror's all about? The thrill, the chase, the delightful terror of being oh-so-wrong, and then, with a gasp, finally stumbling upon the truth.

Chekhov's Gun:

In the world of storytelling, Chekhov's Gun is a concept that's as intriguing as it is simple. It's named after the Russian playwright Anton Chekhov, who famously stated that if you mention a rifle hanging on the wall in the first chapter, it absolutely must go off by the second or third chapter. If it's not going to be fired, it shouldn't be hanging there. It's a principle that's all about the art of foreshadowing and the promise of payoff, and nowhere is it more at home than in the suspenseful and often meticulous realm of horror fiction.

Let's settle in and unpack this concept a bit, shall we? Imagine you're reading a horror novel. In the early pages, the author spends a few sentences describing an old, dusty book of spells hidden in the protagonist's attic. That's not just set dressing; that's Chekhov's Gun. From the moment it's introduced, a promise is made to you, the reader: this book is important, and it's going to matter later. The anticipation of when and how it will come into play becomes a thread that pulls you through the narrative.

Chekhov's Gun doesn't always have to be a physical object, either. It can be a piece of information, a character trait, or even a seemingly throwaway line of dialogue. In horror, this concept is used to build tension and to give the story a sense of inevitable progression toward a climax that feels both surprising and inevitable.

Take, for instance, *Dracula* again. Early on, we learn about the peculiar properties of vampire lore—stakes, garlic, and holy symbols. Stoker doesn't throw in these details haphazardly; they're Chekhov's Guns, each one a promise of future vampire-slaying action. And sure enough, these details come back with a vengeance, quite literally, as the story unfolds. Take a dive into the movie *Jaws* for a second. That part where the shark meets its explosive end thanks to a well-aimed shot at a scuba tank. In real life, scuba tanks don't explode like that. But in the movie, they drop little hints here and there about these tanks (I believe one was a newspaper article, the other a pamphlet, and then of course someone just talking about), and by the time the big moment comes, we're all in. That's the magic of storytelling at work. They use the rule of three, giving us just enough nudge-nudge-winks about those tanks so when the big bang happens, we're buying it. It's a mix of reminding us about the tanks just enough times (that's the rule of three), dropping hints that something big could happen (foreshadowing), and making sure that if something's shown to us, it's going to b e used.

Or consider *The Shining* by Stephen King. The Overlook Hotel itself is a Chekhov's Gun, with its history of violence and mysterious past. Every corridor, every room, every lingering description is a setup, a piece of a puzzle that, when complete, will unleash horror upon the characters and readers alike.

In modern horror, too, Chekhov's Gun is alive and well. In *Bird Box* by Josh Malerman, the creatures that drive people to madness if seen are mentioned early on. This information hangs ominously over the entire narrative, a gun waiting to be fired, and the tension it creates is palpable.

But Chekhov's Gun isn't just about the thrill of the payoff; it's about economy in storytelling. It's a reminder to writers to make every element count, to weave a tight narrative where everything serves a purpose. It's about respecting the reader's attention and not cluttering the story with unnecessary details that don't contribute to the overall tapestry of terror.

In essence, Chekhov's Gun is about the implicit contract between writer and reader: the writer's promise to deliver a meaningful story where every element is there for a reason, and the reader's trust that every setup will have its corresponding moment of revelation. It's a dance of anticipation and fulfillment that, when executed well, can elevate a horror story from simply scary to utterly unforgettable.

So, the next time you're huddled under a blanket, deep into a horror novel, and you come across a detail that the author has taken the time to highlight, take note. That's not just a random piece of information; that's a gun on the wall. And you can bet it's going to go off before the final page is turned.

Foreshadowing:

Foreshadowing is a writer's sneaky way of giving you, the reader, a hint of what's to come without spoiling the surprise. It's like a shadow cast before the event itself, a whisper of future events that tickles the back of your mind as you turn the pages. In horror fiction, foreshadowing is the subtle art of building suspense and setting the stage for the scares ahead.

Picture this: you're wrapped up in a horror story, lost in a world of eerie settings and spine-chilling narratives. The author drops a seemingly innocent comment about an old, forgotten well in the protagonist's new backyard. It's just a part of the landscape, right? But as an astute reader, you get that tingle of anticipation. That well isn't just part of the scenery; it's a harbinger of darker things to come. That is foreshadowing at its finest.

Foreshadowing can take many forms. It might be a character's offhand remark that later takes on a chilling significance, a description of the weather that mirrors the story's mood, or a sense of unease that creeps in during what should be a happy occasion. In horror, these hints can be as subtle as a cold breeze slipping through a crack in the window or as blatant as a character finding a book on ancient curses the day before things start to go inexplicably wrong.

Let's delve into some classic examples. In Shirley Jackson's *The Haunting of Hill House,* the house's very architecture—its twisting hallways and odd angles—foreshadows the disorientation and madness that will envelop the characters. The house itself seems to warn us: within these walls, reality is not what it seems.

In *The Lottery* by Shirley Jackson again, the children gathering stones seems like innocent play, but as the story unfolds, the true purpose of these stones turns that innocence into a gut-wrenching prelude to horror. The casual nature of their collection makes the story's climax all the more shocking.

Modern horror continues to employ foreshadowing with great effect. *In The Girl With All The Gifts* by M.R. Carey, the protagonist's unique appetite and the way others react to her foreshadow a revelation that changes the entire course of the story. The clues are there, laid out for the observant reader to piece together.

Foreshadowing is a dance between the writer and the reader, a game of hide-and-seek with the truth. It requires a delicate balance. Too little, and the twists seem to come from nowhere, leaving the reader feeling cheated. Too much, and the story loses its power to surprise, its ability to shock. When done just right, foreshadowing pulls the reader deeper into the story, creating an engaging experience where every detail is a puzzle piece waiting to find its place in the larger picture. This is why having beta-readers and professional editors are so important, but we'll get to that later on.

In the hands of a skilled horror writer, foreshadowing is a tool that weaves tension and expectation into every page, ensuring that when the horror is finally revealed, it feels as inevitable as it is terrifying. It's the shadow that looms, the whisper that echoes, and the chill that warns of the nightmare to come. And for the reader, it's the delicious dread of knowing that something wicked this way comes.

MacGuffin:

Ah, the MacGuffin—that elusive plot device that drives the characters and the story forward, yet its specific nature is often unimportant to the overall narrative. It's the object, the secret, the thing everyone in the story is chasing after, but for the audience, it's not the 'what' but the 'why' and the 'how' that provide the thrills and chills.

In horror, a MacGuffin can be a powerful tool. It's the ancient artifact that everyone believes will grant unspeakable power, the lost diary that holds the key to a dark mystery, or the cryptic map leading to a place better left undiscovered. The MacGuffin itself isn't necessarily scary, but it's the catalyst for a cascade of events that plunge characters into the heart of darkness.

Take, for instance, the puzzle box in Clive Barker's *Hellraiser*. The box is the MacGuffin that sets the story in motion, but it's not the box's intricate design that holds the real horror; it's what the box opens—a gateway to a realm of pain and suffering presided over by the iconic Pinhead and his Cenobites.

Or consider the videotape in *The Ring*. The tape itself is just an object, but it's the curse associated with it—the inevitable countdown to a ghastly demise after watching it—that fuels the terror. The characters are desperate to understand and, ultimately, to break the curse, driving the narrative toward its eerie conclusion.

The beauty of the MacGuffin lies in its versatility. It's a blank canvas that can take on any form necessary to propel the plot. It's the reason for the haunted house exploration, the monster chase, the descent into the crypt. It's the quest item, but the quest is where the horror lies, not the item itself.

In crafting a horror story with a MacGuffin, the key is to imbue the chase with tension and dread. The MacGuffin must feel worth the characters' risks, even as it leads them into the jaws of nightmare. It's the thing they seek, but around it, the shadows gather, and the unseen horrors watch, waiting.

The MacGuffin is a narrative sleight of hand; while the characters fixate on it, the readers are swept up in the real story—the terrifying journey, the moral quandaries, the ever-present threat. It's not about the MacGuffin itself, but about the horror that the hunt for the MacGuffin unleashes. It's the spark that lights the fire of the story, burning away the mundane to reveal the terror lurking beneath.

Unreliable narrator:

The unreliable narrator—a storyteller whose credibility has been seriously compromised, is a fascinating device in the realm of horror fiction. It's like inviting someone into your home, only to realize they've been subtly rearranging your furniture when you weren't looking. This narrative voice can make the floorboards of a story creak with uncertainty and the walls drip with doubt.

In horror, the unreliable narrator is particularly effective because the genre thrives on the tension between reality and illusion. When the person telling you the story might be as twisted as the tale they're telling, every word is suspect, every motive questionable. It's like walking through a house of mirrors with the lights flickering you can never be quite sure what's real.

Take, for instance, the narrator in Edgar Allan Poe's *The Tell-Tale Heart*. His insistence on his own sanity as he describes the meticulous murder of the old man with the vulture eye only serves to highlight his madness. The horror arises not just from the act of murder, but from the chillingly calm manner in which he narrates it, and the eventual breakdown as the imagined sound of the beating heart drives him to confess.

Or consider *The Haunting of Hill House* again, where Eleanor Vance's perspective is so intertwined with the house's sinister influence that readers are left to wonder how much of her experience is genuine and how much is a product of her unraveling psyche.

The unreliable narrator in horror fiction forces readers to become detectives, sifting through the narrative for clues to what's really happening. It's a game of trust and deception, where the ground is never solid underfoot. This narrator might be hiding the truth, or their perception might be skewed by supernatural forces, trauma, or their own fractured mental state.

What's terrifying about the unreliable narrator is the implication that if you can't trust the story's teller, then the comforting structure of reality itself might be a lie. It's a reminder that our grasp on the 'real' is tenuous at best, and that the mind can be a treacherous place, full of shadows and whispers that can't be trusted.

In the hands of a skilled writer, an unreliable narrator can turn a horror story into a labyrinth with no clear exit. Readers find themselves questioning not just the narrator, but their own interpretations of the unfolding events. It's a powerful way to draw readers into the story, making them complicit in the creation of the horror. After all, if you can't trust the narrator, the only thing left to trust is your own sense of dread.

In Medias Res:

Ever walked into a movie theater just a tad late? The story's already rolling, the characters are in the thick of it, and you're scrambling to catch up. That's a bit like the storytelling technique called "In Medias Res," a fancy Latin term that means "in the midst of things."

When authors use In Medias Res, they're dropping us right into the action, bypassing the slow climb of the story mountain and instead starting us off at a sprint. It's like being thrown into the deep end of a pool and having to figure out how to swim. It's exhilarating, a bit disorienting, and totally hooks your attention. A perfect example is a book I published, *Eight Cylinders* by Jason Parent.

So why do writers do this? Well, it's a brilliant way to grab readers by the collar and pull them into the narrative. Instead of beginning with a long-winded introduction, setting the scene, and then, maybe a few chapters in, getting to the good stuff, In Medias Res puts the good stuff front and center. It's like saying, "Hey, you're in my world now, and look, things are already happening!"

But it's not just about the shock value or the adrenaline rush. Starting In Medias Res can set the tone for the entire story. It can give us a glimpse of the drama, the stakes, and the characters in a way that's immediate and compelling. Plus, it can create a delicious sense of mystery. We're playing catch-up, trying to piece together the hows and whys, and that puzzle can be really engaging.

In horror fiction, this technique can be especially potent. Imagine opening a book and the first thing you read is a scene of heart-pounding terror. You don't know why the characters are in danger, you don't know what's after them, but you want to find out. And just like that, you're hooked.

But it's not all about the shock and awe. In Medias Res can also be a tool for pacing. By starting in the middle, the story has a built-in momentum that can carry readers along. And as the narrative unfolds, the past can be revealed in layers, which can be a more natural and intriguing way to discover a character's backstory or the events leading up to the main plot.

Of course, like any technique, it has to be done right. If you're too disorienting, readers might feel lost. If you don't eventually fill in the gaps, they might feel cheated. It's a balancing act, giving just enough to keep readers on the edge of their seats, but not so much that they fall off.

In the end, In Medias Res is about making an entrance. It's the author saying, "Forget easing into the pool; let's make a splash." And when done well, it's a splash that can carry the reader all the way to the last page, surfacing only after the full story has been told.

Jump Scare:

Jump scares. They're the bread and butter of horror movies, those moments that send popcorn flying and hearts racing. But can a book, without the aid of a screeching soundtrack and sudden visual shocks, really make you jump? Absolutely. The art of the jump scare in literature is a crafty blend of timing, misdirection, and the reader's own imagination.

In movies, a jump scare is all about the unexpected—a sudden loud noise or a ghastly face flashing on screen. In books, it's a bit different. It's about the unexpected twist of words, the sudden revelation, the thing that shouldn't be there but is. It's a narrative leap out of the shadows that makes your pulse quicken.

The secret to a successful jump scare in fiction is the buildup. It's the quiet moments, the slow ratcheting up of tension, the feeling that something is not quite right. Authors weave a tapestry of suspense, drawing readers into a false sense of security. And then, when you least expect it—bam—they hit you with a scare.

But how exactly does an author craft such a moment without visual aids? It's all about the power of suggestion. The human mind is wonderfully adept at filling in the blanks. A writer might describe the soft creak of a floorboard, the sudden chill in the air, or the faintest whisper of a voice when there should be silence. The reader's brain does the rest, conjuring up horrors far more terrifying than anything that could be explicitly described.

Another tool in the writer's kit is the abrupt, short sentence that follows a long, descriptive passage. You're lulled into a rhythm by the prose, and then a sentence hits you like a cold hand from the dark. It's the literary equivalent of the monster jumping out of the closet.

It's all about the timing.

But a jump scare in a book isn't just about the moment of terror; it's about the aftermath. The best scares linger. They make you hesitant to turn the page, to read on. They make you question the shadows in your own room. Because once an author has successfully made you jump, they've also made the horror personal. It's no longer confined to the page; it's in your head.

In essence, jump scares in fiction rely on the dance between author and reader, a choreography that plays with anticipation and the fear of the unknown. It's a testament to the power of words and imagination, proving that a well-crafted sentence can be just as heart-stopping as any movie scare. And unlike a film, where the scare is over as soon as the scene cuts, a book's scare can make you apprehensive about every line that follows, turning each page into a potential trapdoor into the abyss.

For me, jump scares in movies often rub me the wrong way. They can come across as a bit of a cheap thrill, a low-hanging fruit for quick scares. But in a book? That's a whole different story. When I come across a jump scare on the page, it's a visceral reaction. I find myself tucking my feet up, casting a wary glance over my shoulder, and silently tipping my hat to the author for pulling one over on me so skillfully.

The Mirror Character:

In the realm of horror fiction, the concept of the Mirror Character stands as a fascinating and often underappreciated tool in an author's arsenal. This literary device involves creating a character that reflects, contrasts, or parallels the protagonist, offering a deeper insight into their psyche, choices, and moral compass. The mirror character is more than just a foil or an adversary; they are a reflection of what the protagonist could become or what they once were, serving as a critical element in the narrative's thematic exploration.

At its core, the mirror character is about juxtaposition and reflection. They are often crafted to share similarities with the protagonist but diverge in key choices or moral standings. This contrast is not just for dramatic effect; it's a deliberate choice to highlight the protagonist's journey, struggles, and potential paths. In horror, where characters often grapple with internal and external demons, the mirror character can embody the protagonist's worst fears, unfulfilled desires, or repressed aspects of their personality.

In horror literature, mirror characters are used to great effect. For instance, in Mary Shelley's *Frankenstein*, the Creature can be seen as a mirror to Victor Frankenstein. Both share feelings of isolation and a quest for understanding, yet their choices set them on vastly different paths. The Creature's actions and experiences hold up a mirror to Victor's own moral failings and the consequences of his unchecked ambition.

Another example is found in Stephen King's *The Shining*. Jack Torrance and the Overlook Hotel act as mirror characters to each other. The hotel's malevolent presence amplifies Jack's own inner demons, reflecting his struggles with addiction and violence. This mirroring escalates the horror, as it blurs the lines between the supernatural and the psychological, making the terror all the more personal and real.

Creating an effective mirror character requires a delicate balance. They must be similar enough to the protagonist to create a meaningful reflection but different enough to provide a clear contrast. This character should challenge the protagonist's beliefs and decisions, forcing them to confront aspects of themselves they might rather ignore. In horror, this confrontation often leads to critical moments of tension and revelation, adding depth to both the story and the characters involved.

In horror, the mirror character often embodies the genre's central themes, such as the nature of evil, the duality of the human psyche, or the consequences of one's actions. They serve as a living, breathing embodiment of the story's moral and thematic questions. By interacting with, or in some cases, battling against their mirror, the protagonist is forced to confront their own fears and flaws, making their journey more compelling and the story's resolution more impactful.

The mirror character is a powerful tool in horror fiction, offering a unique way to explore complex themes and deepen character development. By reflecting the protagonist's inner world, these characters illuminate the heart of the story, making the horror more than just a series of frightening events, but a journey into the depths of the human soul. As authors weave these mirrored narratives, they invite readers to look beyond the surface scares and delve into the reflective waters of the human condition.

Juxtaposition:

Juxtaposition in horror fiction is like a masterful stroke in a dark painting, where contrasting elements are placed side by side to create a striking effect. This literary technique involves placing dissimilar characters, settings, or themes together to highlight their differences. It's like setting a candle in the dark; the light seems brighter, and the shadows, deeper. In horror, juxtaposition can turn an ordinary scene into something chilling, making the reader's heart race a little faster.

Imagine a scene where a cheerful, sunlit playground sits next to an old, creepy cemetery. The innocence of the playground, with its laughter and light, stands in stark contrast to the somber, eerie quiet of the cemetery. This contrast doesn't just paint a vivid picture; it creates a sense of unease. It's this unease, this feeling that something isn't quite right, that lies at the heart of horror. Juxtaposition plays with our expectations and emotions, making the horror elements stand out even more.

Horror stories often use juxtaposition to enhance the sense of dread. For example, a story might contrast the normalcy of everyday life with sudden, inexplicable horror. This can be seen in Stephen King's *It*, where the innocence of childhood is set against the backdrop of an ancient, malevolent entity preying on the town's children. The normalcy of the children's lives makes the horror of what they face even more striking.

Another way juxtaposition is used is through characters. A kind, gentle character might be contrasted with a brutal, violent antagonist. This not only highlights the evil of the antagonist but also the vulnerability and courage of the protagonist. It's a dance of light and dark, where each step of one reveals more about the other.

To use juxtaposition effectively, it's important to choose elements that are truly contrasting. The key is in the details. It's not just about putting a scary scene next to a happy one; it's about finding elements that, when placed together, change the way we see both. It's like adding a pinch of salt to a sweet dish; the salt doesn't just add its flavor, it enhances the sweetness.

Why does this matter? Juxtaposition adds depth to the story. It's not just about scaring the reader; it's about making them feel something more. By contrasting horror with normalcy, innocence with evil, or hope with despair, authors can create a more immersive and emotionally engaging experience. It's this emotional engagement that makes a horror story memorable, lingering in the reader's mind long after the last page is turned.

When done well, it can turn a simple tale into a complex, emotionally rich experience. It's a reminder that sometimes, the most effective way to illuminate the darkness is by placing it next to the light.

Flashbacks:

Flashbacks in horror fiction are like peering through a dusty, cobweb-laden window into the past. They're not just a storytelling technique—they're a portal that takes your reader back in time, revealing secrets, backstory, and often, the root of all the spooky stuff happening in the present.

Imagine you're reading a horror novel. The protagonist is wandering through an eerily silent house, and suddenly, they find an old photograph. This isn't just any photo. It's a gateway to a flashback. Bit cliché, but suddenly, you're not in the present anymore. You're witnessing events from years ago, events that explain why the house is more than just a building. It's a character, haunted by its past.

Flashbacks are like the secret sauce in horror. They add depth to your story, giving context to the terror. They answer the 'whys' that keep readers flipping pages. Why is this house haunted? Why does that character never go into the basement? It's all in the flashbacks.

But here's the thing: flashbacks are a bit like spice. Too little, and your story might feel flat. Too much, and you risk losing your reader in a tangle of timelines. The key is balance. Use flashbacks to enhance the story, not overshadow it. They should be like ghostly whispers, not screaming banshees.

And remember, flashbacks are not just about dumping information. They're an opportunity to build suspense, develop characters, and create a richer, more layered narrative. Think of them as a puzzle piece that, when placed correctly, makes the whole picture clearer and more intriguing. Timing is very important with flashbacks. Only reveal the information to the reader exactly when it's needed. Not too early. Not too late.

In horror, flashbacks can be especially powerful. They can reveal a character's traumatic past, uncover dark secrets, or provide chilling context to a cursed object. They're a tool to build empathy, too. When readers understand the 'why,' they connect more deeply with the 'what's happening now.'

So, when you're writing your next horror masterpiece, consider how flashbacks can add to your story. Use them wisely, and you'll not only scare your readers but also give them a story that haunts them long after they've turned the last page. Remember, in horror, the past is never really dead. It's just waiting in the shadows, ready to be revisited.

Misdirection:

Misdirection in horror fiction is like a magician's sleight of hand, but instead of playing with cards, you're playing with your reader's expectations. It's a crafty technique where you lead your audience down one path, only to surprise them with something entirely different. This twist not only adds an element of surprise but also deepens the intrigue and horror of your story.

Think of it as setting up a trail of breadcrumbs. Your readers follow these, thinking they know where the story is heading. They're anticipating one thing, but then, bam! You reveal something entirely unexpected, and suddenly, the story takes on a new, more thrilling dimension.

Imagine you're writing a story about a series of mysterious disappearances in a small town. The narrative initially points to an ancient curse linked to an old, abandoned mansion on the outskirts of the town. As the story progresses, clues suggest that the mansion is the epicenter of the disappearances.

However, in a twist, it's revealed that the true cause of the disappearances is not supernatural at all but the work of a very human antagonist with a personal vendetta against the town. This revelation should be shocking yet believable, with earlier subtle clues now making perfect sense.

By mastering the art of misdirection, you can keep your readers on the edge of their seats, constantly guessing and re-evaluating what they know about your story. It's a powerful tool in horror fiction, one that can turn a good story into an unforgettable journey.

The Uncanny Valley:

The term "Uncanny Valley" might sound like a mysterious place in a horror novel, but it's actually a concept that explains why certain things creep us out. Originally from robotics and 3D animation, the uncanny valley refers to the eerie feeling we get when something is almost human, but not quite right. This concept has been brilliantly adapted into horror fiction, adding an extra layer of creepiness to stories.

Imagine a doll that looks almost like a real child, but its eyes are just a bit too glassy, or its movements are slightly jerky. That's the uncanny valley in action. It's that unsettling feeling you can't quite put your finger on, the sense that something is off, but you don't know what. This feeling plays a huge role in horror, where the slightly-off can be more terrifying than the blatantly monstrous.

In literature, authors use the uncanny valley to create a sense of dread and unease. It's not just about making something look or act almost human—it's about tapping into our deepest fears of what lies beneath the surface of the familiar. This can be seen in characters like Frankenstein's monster or the eerily lifelike automatons in some Gothic tales.

Why It Works:

- Primal Fear: The uncanny valley taps into our primal fears. Something that looks human but isn't quite can trigger a deep-seated alarm in our brains, warning us of something unnatural.

- Disturbingly Familiar: The power of the uncanny valley in horror fiction lies in its ability to take the familiar and twist it just enough to become disturbing. This plays with our expectations and makes the ordinary suddenly threatening.

- Psychological Horror: It's not just about physical appearances. The uncanny valley can also apply to behaviors and emotions. Characters who exhibit almost-human emotions or reactions can be deeply unsettling, adding a psychological twist to the horror. What a great way to pull the reader into the story at a psychological level.

Using the Uncanny Valley in Writing:

When writing horror, you can use the uncanny valley to create an atmosphere of suspense and unease. Describe a character or object in detail, highlighting aspects that are nearly human but subtly wrong. Focus on the reactions of your characters to these uncanny elements—their fear and confusion can amplify the horror for the reader.

A great example in history is of a family who had witnesses a UFO. A few days later two men showed up at their door, dressed in black, but acting...strange. They just looked off. Their skin pale, almost stretchy. They asked weird questions, said they'd be back, and left. Apparently they visited another house not too far away, but were never heard from again.

Remember, the key to effectively using the uncanny valley in horror fiction is subtlety. It's the slight deviations from the norm, the almost imperceptible wrongness, that truly unsettle the reader. By mastering this, you can turn an ordinary horror story into a deeply disturbing journey into the uncanny.

Doppelganger:

The concept of the doppelganger, a German term meaning "double walker," has long fascinated storytellers and audiences alike. In literature, particularly in horror and psychological thrillers, doppelgangers are used to explore themes of identity, the unconscious mind, and the uncanny. Let's delve into the eerie world of doppelgangers and their significance in fiction.

- The Essence of Doppelgangers:
  A doppelganger in fiction is typically a look-alike or double of a protagonist, often embodying the opposite traits of the character they mirror. This double can be a physical twin, a spiritual manifestation, or even a metaphorical representation of a hidden aspect of the main

character's personality. The use of a doppelganger allows authors to delve deep into the psyche of their characters, presenting internal conflicts and hidden fears in a tangible form.

- Symbolism and Themes:
Doppelgangers often symbolize the inner turmoil or the darker side of a character. They can represent repressed desires, guilt, or aspects of the self that the protagonist is afraid to acknowledge. In horror fiction, the doppelganger can be a source of terror, embodying the unknown and the uncanny. They challenge the protagonist's sense of self and reality, leading to intense psychological conflict.

- Doppelgangers in Horror Fiction:
In horror, the doppelganger trope is used to evoke fear and suspense. The appearance of a double can signify impending doom or a descent into madness. Classic examples include Edgar Allan Poe's "William Wilson" short story, where the doppelganger represents the protagonist's conscience, and Stephen King's "The Outsider," where the doppelganger is a malevolent entity. For a truly unique domestic thriller experience, be sure to read *The Face You Wear* by Faith Pierce.

- Psychological Implications:
Psychologically, doppelgangers can be interpreted as manifestations of the Jungian shadow—the unacknowledged and often rejected aspects of the self. They force characters to confront parts of themselves they have denied or suppressed, leading to either self-awareness or self-destruction.

- Modern Interpretations:
In contemporary fiction, doppelgangers are used not just for horror but also to explore existential themes. They can question the nature of identity and reality, as seen in films like *Us* by Jordan Peele, where the

doppelgangers represent a suppressed class uprising.

In conclusion, the doppelganger is a powerful and versatile trope in fiction, especially in horror. It serves as a mirror to the protagonist, reflecting hidden truths and fears. Whether used to evoke terror, explore psychological depths, or question existential realities, the doppelganger remains a compelling and enduring element in storytelling, captivating readers with its eerie resonance and multifaceted symbolism.

Pacing and Rhythm:

Pacing and rhythm in writing are like the heartbeat of a story. They determine the speed at which a narrative unfolds and the flow of the words on the page. Mastering these elements can transform a good story into a compelling, unputdownable read. Let's explore how to effectively use pacing and rhythm in your writing.

1. Understanding Pacing
   - Pacing Defined: Pacing is the speed at which a story progresses. It's about how quickly or slowly events unfold and how much time is spent on different parts of the story.

   - Variety is Key: A well-paced story will vary its tempo. Fast pacing is used in action scenes or climactic moments, while slower pacing can be used for character development or setting the scene.

   - Impact of Pacing: Pacing affects how readers engage with the story. Too fast, and important details might be missed; too slow, and the reader might lose interest.

2. Techniques to Control Pacing

- Sentence Structure: Short, choppy sentences can speed up the pace, creating tension or urgency. Longer, more complex sentences slow down the pace, allowing for reflection or detail.

- Paragraph and Chapter Length: Short paragraphs and chapters can quicken the pace, while longer ones can slow it down.

- Dialogue vs. Description: Rapid-fire dialogue can accelerate pacing, while lengthy descriptions tend to slow it down.

3. Rhythm in Writing

- Rhythm Defined: Rhythm is the pattern of sounds and silences in writing. It's about the musicality and flow of the words.

- Creating Rhythm: Use a mix of sentence lengths and structures to create a pleasing rhythm. Pay attention to the sound of words and the flow of sentences.

- Read Aloud: Reading your work aloud can help you hear the rhythm and identify any awkward or jarring spots. Better yet, have someone read it to you.

4. Balancing Pacing and Rhythm

- Consistency vs. Variation: While consistency in pacing and rhythm can provide stability, variation can keep readers engaged. Find the right balance for your story.

- Genre Considerations: Different genres have different pacing expectations. Thrillers often have a fast pace, while literary fiction might take a slower, more measured approach.

- Reader Engagement: Use pacing and rhythm to control how your reader experiences the story. Build up to climactic moments with faster pacing, and allow for reflection with slower sections.

5. Pacing and Rhythm in Different Story Elements
  - Action Scenes: Use quick pacing and short, sharp sentences.

  - Emotional Scenes: Slow down the pace to let the reader feel the character's emotions. Use rhythm to enhance the mood.

  - Exposition and Description: Balance is key. Don't let the pace drag, but give enough detail to immerse the reader.

Pacing and rhythm are essential tools in a writer's arsenal. They shape the reader's experience and are crucial for maintaining engagement throughout the story. By mastering these elements, you can guide your readers through the ebbs and flows of your narrative, keeping them hooked from the first page to the last. Remember, the pace and rhythm of your story are not just about the events that happen, but how you choose to tell them.

Rule of three:

We've covered this a bit earlier in the book, but let's take a more detailed look at the rule of three.

In the world of storytelling, certain principles have stood the test of time, resonating across cultures and epochs. Among these, the Rule of Three shines as a beacon of narrative efficacy. This principle suggests that ideas, concepts, or elements presented in threes are inherently more captivating, satisfying, and memorable. It's a pattern deeply ingrained in human psychology, evident in our folklore, literature, and even daily communication.

The essence of the Rule of Three lies in its simplicity and rhythmic harmony. It theorizes that when things come in threes, they strike a chord that is both familiar and pleasing to the human mind. This pattern creates a natural rhythm that is easy for the brain to process and remember. From the three little pigs to the three musketeers, the Rule of Three has been a staple in storytelling, offering a structure that audiences find instinctively compelling. It's why most great emails and letters always have three sections/paragraphs.

In writing, the applications of the Rule of Three are manifold. It can be seen in the development of characters, where introducing a character through three key traits or actions creates a well-rounded and memorable persona. In the realm of plot, the three-act structure (beginning, middle, end) is a testament to the enduring power of this rule, providing a framework that balances exposition, conflict, and resolution in a harmonious dance.

The Rule of Three also finds its place in the subtle art of repetition. By repeating an idea or theme three times, writers can emphasize its importance, etching it into the reader's memory (remember when talked about Jaws earlier). This technique is particularly potent in genres like suspense or horror, where the first two instances set the stage for tension, and the third delivers the climax or twist, often with chilling effectiveness.

However, the magic of the Rule of Three isn't just in its ability to structure and emphasize; it's also a key player in the realm of humor. In comedy, setting up a pattern with the first two items and then breaking it with the third creates a surprise or twist that triggers laughter, a technique used masterfully by comedians and writers alike.

Despite its power, the Rule of Three is not without its pitfalls. Overuse can render writing predictable and formulaic. The key lies in balancing its use with other narrative techniques, and sometimes, in subverting the rule itself to create an element of surprise. This delicate balancing act ensures that the story remains engaging and the audience stays invested.

From classic fairy tales to modern cinema, the Rule of Three has proven its worth as a storytelling tool. It leverages our brain's preference for patterns, making stories more engaging, memorable, and satisfying. Whether in the crafting of a novel, a screenplay, or even a speech, incorporating the Rule of Three can add rhythm, emphasis, and impact to storytelling. Yet, the true art lies in using it judiciously and creatively, enhancing the narrative without making it a slave to formula. In the hands of a skilled writer, the Rule of Three is not just a rule but a gateway to the realm of timeless storytelling.

Elements of Fiction (literary techniques)

Allegory:

Allegory in horror is like a secret message woven into a spooky tale. It's more than just a story about ghosts or monsters; it's a deeper commentary on real-world issues, hidden beneath the surface of the narrative. Think of it as a puzzle, where the horror elements represent something larger, like societal fears, moral dilemmas, or human nature.

For instance, a story about a haunted house might not just be about the ghosts. It could be an allegory for the lingering effects of past traumas or unresolved family issues. The house, with its creaky floors and hidden rooms, becomes a symbol of the mind, with its hidden fears and secrets.

We're all familiar with the zombie allegory, perfectly portrayed in George A. Romero's *Dawn of the Dead* movie.

Allegory in horror allows authors to explore complex themes in an engaging, often chilling way. It invites readers to look beyond the surface scares and consider the underlying message. This deeper layer adds richness to the story, making it not just a thrilling ride but also a thought-provoking experience.

It is a clever blend of entertainment and introspection. A way of using the thrill of fear to shine a light on the darker aspects of our world and ourselves, making the horror genre not just about frights, but also about insights.

Symbolism:

Symbolism is a powerful literary tool, especially potent in the realm of horror fiction. It's like a secret language, where objects, characters, or events represent something beyond their literal meaning, adding layers of depth and complexity to a story. In horror, symbolism often serves to amplify the themes, emotions, and underlying messages, making the experience richer and more haunting for th e reader.

In horror, common symbols might include darkness representing the unknown, blood symbolizing life or death, or a decaying house mirroring a character's mental state. These symbols aren't just there for show—they're carefully chosen to enhance the story's mood and meaning. For example, a storm could symbolize approaching danger or internal turmoil, adding a layer of foreboding to the narrative (we'll cover more examples later on when we learn about creating settings).

Symbolism in horror works because it engages the reader's imagination, inviting them to look beyond the surface. It's not just about a character walking through a dark forest. It's about what that forest represents: fear, the unknown, or a journey into the subconscious. This engagement makes the horror more personal and impactful, as readers find their interpretations and connections.

Moreover, symbolism can provide a sense of universality to horror stories. Symbols like shadows, mirrors, or the moon have deep-rooted meanings in various cultures, tapping into shared human fears and experiences. This universality makes the horror resonate on a deeper level, transcending the immediate scare to leave a lasting impression.

Symbolism in horror is about weaving a web of deeper meaning beneath the surface scares. It's a way for authors to communicate complex ideas and emotions subtly, enriching the narrative and making the horror about more than just the fear; it's about the human experience reflected in those fears.

Irony:

Irony is like a wink from the author, a clever twist where things aren't quite as they seem. It's when the opposite of what you expect happens, and it can turn a story on its head, adding depth, humor, or poignancy. Let's explore how irony weaves its magic in fiction, with a few classic examples.

The Three Faces of Irony:

- Verbal Irony: This is when someone says one thing but means another. It's like sarcasm's more sophisticated cousin. For instance, in Jane Austen's *Pride and Prejudice*, when Mr. Bennet dryly remarks that Mr. Collins' letter is "the work of a moment," he's subtly poking fun at its long-windedness. It might not be horror, but there are so many things authors can learn from this book.

- Situational Irony: Here, the situation itself is ironic. It's like life playing a practical joke. In O. Henry's "The Gift of the Magi," a young couple sells their most prized possessions to buy each other gifts, only to find the gifts are now useless. It's a touching twist that highlights their love and sacrifice.

- Dramatic Irony: This happens when the audience knows something the characters don't. It's like being in on a secret. Shakespeare loved this one. In *Romeo and Juliet*, we know Juliet isn't really dead, but Romeo doesn't, leading to tragic consequences.

Irony can serve various purposes in a story:

- Adding Humor: Irony can be a source of laughter, especially when characters find themselves in absurd or contradictory situations.

- Creating Suspense: Knowing something the characters don't can keep readers on the edge of their seats, eagerly anticipating the moment of revelation.

- Highlighting Themes: Irony can underscore a story's deeper meanings or themes, often in a subtle and thought-provoking way.

- Enhancing Character Development: Characters' reactions to ironic situations can reveal their true nature or lead to significant growth.

Classic Examples:

- "The Story of an Hour" by Kate Chopin: The protagonist feels a sense of freedom after hearing of her husband's death, only for him to return home alive, leading to her own death. The irony is both tragic and a commentary on the constraints of marriage.

- *Animal Farm* by George Orwell: The animals overthrow their human oppressor, only to end up with a regime just as oppressive. It's a stark, ironic commentary on the nature of power and revolution.

Irony is a powerful tool in the hands of a skilled writer. It can add layers of meaning, create emotional impact, and engage readers in a unique way. Whether it's through a witty remark (don't you just love a witty character?), a surprising twist, or a dramatic revelation, irony enriches a narrative, making it more engaging and memorable. In the world of fiction, sometimes it's the unexpected turns that make the journey most worthwhile.

Imagery:

Imagery in fiction is the art of using vivid and descriptive language to create mental images for the reader. It's not just about visual pictures; imagery encompasses all five senses – sight, sound, smell, taste, and touch. This literary device is crucial in immersing readers into the world of the story, making them feel as if they are part of the scene.

A skilled author uses imagery to bring settings and characters to life. For instance, describing the musty scent of an old library, the rough texture of a tree's bark, or the distant sound of church bells in a quiet village. These sensory details help readers to experience the story's environment in a more intimate and tangible way.

Imagery also plays a significant role in evoking emotions and setting the mood. A dark, stormy night can set a tone of foreboding, while a bright, sunny meadow can evoke feelings of joy and peace. It's a powerful tool in creating an emotional connection between the story and the reader.

Moreover, imagery can be symbolic, adding deeper meaning to the narrative. For example, a wilting flower might symbolize the end of a character's youth, or a raging storm could represent internal turmoil.

In summary, imagery is a key element in fiction that enriches the narrative. It transforms words on a page into a vivid, sensory experience, deepening the reader's engagement with the story and enhancing the overall impact of the tale. Just be careful of being too flowery, especially in the horror genre. By reading enough modern horror books and new releases, you'll know exactly where the right balance is, which will help reinforce your own, unique voice. We'll talk about imagery later on again.

> The end of one story is just the beginning of another. Every finished book is a stepping stone to your next adventure.

Simile:

Simile, a fundamental device in the writer's toolkit, is a figure of speech that draws a comparison between two different things, explicitly using the words "like" or "as." This literary technique is a cornerstone of creative expression, allowing authors to paint vivid pictures in the minds of their readers, enriching their narrative with depth and relatability.

The beauty of a simile lies in its ability to connect the familiar with the unfamiliar, making abstract or complex ideas more tangible and understandable. For instance, saying "her smile was like sunshine" not only describes the smile but also evokes feelings of warmth and happiness associated with sunshine. This comparison helps readers visualize and emotionally connect with the text.

Similes also serve to enhance the reader's experience by adding rhythm and beauty to the prose. They can create a lyrical quality in writing, making the text more enjoyable and memorable. However, the effectiveness of a simile depends on its originality and relevance. Overused similes can feel clichéd and may detract from the impact of the writing.

Similes are a powerful literary device that, when used skillfully, can transform simple descriptions into vivid, emotive, and engaging imagery, enriching the reader's experience and deepening their connection to the text.

Metaphor:

We'll take a deep dive into this when we get to writing descriptions, but for now, a metaphor is a literary device that directly compares two unrelated subjects, asserting that one is the other, unlike a simile which uses "like" or "as" for comparison. This technique enriches language, providing depth and new perspectives to writing. Metaphors are powerful tools in storytelling, capable of conveying complex emotions and ideas succinctly. For example, describing time as a "thief" suggests its stealthy, irreversible nature, encapsulating a profound concept in a simple phrase. Effective metaphors can illuminate and transform the ordinary, offering readers fresh insights into everyday experiences, making them a staple of expressive and impactful writing.

Personification:

Personification is a literary device that breathes life into the inanimate, bestowing human qualities upon non-human entities. This technique is more than a mere decorative tool; it's a bridge connecting readers to the abstract and the intangible, making the unfamiliar familiar. By attributing human characteristics to objects, animals, or even abstract ideas, personification enriches the narrative, making it more relatable and vivid.

In literature, personification allows for a deeper emotional connection with the reader. For instance, when a storm is described as "angry," it does more than depict the weather; it conveys a mood, setting an emotional tone that resonates with the reader. Similarly, when time is said to "crawl," it personifies time, emphasizing the slow passage experienced during a tedious or anxious mom ent.

This device is particularly effective in creating imagery that sticks with the reader. It transforms the environment of a story into an active participant, often reflecting the internal state of characters or the thematic essence of the narrative.

Moreover, personification can be a powerful tool in poetry, where emotions and abstract concepts often take center stage. It allows poets to convey complex emotions and ideas in a tangible way, making abstract concepts graspable and emotionally impactful.

However, the use of personification requires a delicate balance. Overuse or overly whimsical personification can detract from the seriousness of a narrative or confuse the reader. *Especially* in horror fiction. When used sensibly, it can illuminate and deepen the reader's understanding and emotional engagement with the text.

Hyperbole:

Hyperbole, the art of deliberate and dramatic exaggeration, serves as a powerful tool in the author's toolkit, infusing language with emotion, humor, and emphasis. Far from mere overstatement, hyperbole is a deliberate, poetic, and often playful way to convey feelings and impressions that might otherwise be too complex or subtle for plain language.

In literature, hyperbole amplifies a sentiment or situation to such an extent that it becomes vividly memorable. For instance, saying "I've told you a million times" doesn't literally mean a million repetitions, but it effectively conveys the speaker's frustration and the repetitive nature of the situation. This kind of exaggeration can inject humor, add emphasis, or express strong emotions in a way that resonates with readers.

Hyperbole also plays a significant role in character development. A character prone to hyperbole might be seen as dramatic, passionate, or even unreliable, adding layers to their personality and interactions. It can also highlight the intensity of a character's experience or emotions, making their inner world more accessible and relatable to the reader.

In poetry and prose, hyperbole can elevate the ordinary to the extraordinary, transforming mundane descriptions into vivid, imaginative landscapes. It allows writers to play with reality, stretching it to create a heightened sense of importance or urgency, or to imbue a narrative with a fantastical or surreal quality.

However, the effectiveness of hyperbole lies in its judicious use. Overuse or inappropriate use can lead to a loss of credibility or seriousness, or can render the text melodramatic. When used with care, it can be a powerful way to convey emotions, create emphasis, and add a layer of depth and creativity to writing.

Through hyperbole, writers can paint with broad strokes, capturing the essence of their thoughts and feelings in a way that is larger than life, and all the more truthful for it.

Conclusion to section 1

As we close this exploration into the foundations of horror and dark fiction, it's evident that this genre, like the creatures and specters that populate its pages, is a living entity, constantly evolving and adapting. From its ancient roots to its modern manifestations, horror has always been a reflection of humanity's deepest fears, hopes, and the societal zeitgeist of its times.

The history of horror literature offers a fascinating journey, charting not just the evolution of a genre, but also the changing landscapes of human society. Each era, from the medieval tales of dread to the post-modern explorations of the human psyche, has contributed layers of complexity and nuance to the genre. These historical touchstones serve as a reminder that while the nature of our fears may change, the need to confront and understand them remains a constant.

Our exploration of the various sub-genres and key elements has underscored the richness and diversity of horror. The myriad tropes and motifs, from haunted mansions to vengeful spirits, are not mere storytelling tools but are emblematic of universal themes and emotions. They resonate because they tap into fundamental human experiences, whether it's the fear of the unknown or the complexities of the human mind.

Yet, as we've discussed, the true power of horror lies not just in its ability to terrify, but in its capacity to reflect. It holds up a mirror to society, to individuals, and asks probing questions. It challenges perceptions, subverts expectations, and often, offers catharsis. For writers, understanding these foundational elements is crucial. It equips them with the tools to craft stories that are not only spine-chilling but also deeply meaningful.

In the end, horror and dark fiction, with its rich tapestry of history, its diverse sub-genres, and its foundational elements, serves as a testament to humanity's enduring fascination with the macabre. It's a genre that celebrates the thrill of the unknown, the allure of the forbidden, and the complexities of the human condition. As we venture forth, whether as readers or writers, let's carry forward the lessons, inspirations, and insights gleaned from this exploration, using them to illuminate the shadowy corners of our imagination and the world around us.

Section 2: Crafting Characters

In the eerie and mysterious world of horror and dark fiction, characters are the lifeblood that makes everything pulse with excitement and fear. Think of them as the friends (or foes) guiding you through haunted mansions, foggy, cursed towns, and the twisty turns of their own minds. They're the ones who make a story feel real and gripping, pulling us into the narrative and helping us navigate the spooky and unpredictable waters of horror.

At its heart, horror is all about what it means to be human—our deepest fears, our brightest hopes, our weaknesses, and our strengths. It's through characters that these big ideas come to life. Whether it's the final girl fighting back against all odds, a character grappling with their own demons, or an ordinary person facing extraordinary horrors, it's their stories, their battles, and their victories that stick with us and make the scares feel real.

Creating characters that stay with readers isn't easy. They need to be complex, believable, and someone we can relate to, even in the wildest of tales. They should make us feel something, make us think, and reflect the real people we know in our lives. In this section, we're going to dive into how to build these kinds of characters in horror and dark fiction. We'll look at different types of characters, what drives them, and how they change over time, uncovering the secrets to creating characters that haunt our thoughts long after we've finished the story.

Remember, your characters are the heart of your story. They connect your fictional world to the reader's reality. Through them, the abstract fears and themes in horror take shape, making the scares more intense and the darkness more profound. So, let's step into the shoes of these characters, getting to know their hearts, their minds, and the eerie worlds they call home.

Chapter 1

Iconic Characters in Horror Literature

Horror literature has given birth to a pantheon of memorable characters that have not only defined the genre but have also seeped into the broader cultural consciousness. These characters, with their unique blend of relatability, terror, and complexity, serve as benchmarks for writers and readers alike. Let's delve into some of the most iconic figures in horror literature, exploring their depths and understanding their lasting impact.

- Count Dracula (from *Dracula* by Bram Stoker): Perhaps the most iconic vampire in literature, Count Dracula embodies the fears of the unknown and the allure of the forbidden. His suave demeanor juxtaposed with his predatory nature makes him a character of contrasts, representing both the allure and danger of the unknown.

- Victor Frankenstein & The Monster (from *Frankenstein* by Mary Shelley): Victor's ambition and his monstrous creation's quest for identity and acceptance delve deep into themes of creation, responsibility, and the consequences of playing god. The Monster, often misunderstood, is a poignant figure of isolation and longing.

- Jack Torrance (from *The Shining* by Stephen King): A tragic figure, Jack's descent into madness in the haunted Overlook Hotel is a chilling exploration of the fragility of the human mind. His internal struggles, exacerbated by supernatural forces, make him both a sympathetic and terrifying character.

- Norman Bates (from *Psycho* by Robert Bloch): Norman's dual nature, influenced by his domineering mother, delves into the dark recesses of the human psyche. His character is a study in duality, obsession, and the blurred lines between sanity and madness.

- Roderick Usher (from *The Fall of the House of Usher* by Edgar Allan Poe): Roderick, with his acute sensitivity and impending doom, embodies the Gothic tradition's themes of decay, madness, and ancestral curses.

- Cthulhu (from *The Call of Cthulhu* by H.P. Lovecraft): This cosmic entity represents the insignificance of humanity in the vastness of the cosmos. Cthulhu, with its incomprehensible form and power, epitomizes Lovecraft's themes of cosmic horror and the unknown.

- Carrie White (from *Carrie* by Stephen King): A tormented teenager with telekinetic powers, Carrie's tragic tale is one of bullying, societal pressures, and the explosive consequences of suppressed rage.

- Dorian Gray (from *The Picture of Dorian Gray* by Oscar Wilde): Dorian's eternal youth, juxtaposed with his portrait's decaying visage, delves into themes of vanity, morality, and the cost of unchecked hedonism.

- Annie Wilkes (from *Misery* by Stephen King): Annie is a chilling portrayal of obsession. As a "number one fan" of writer Paul Sheldon, her volatile mix of care and cruelty toward her captive author is a deep dive into the dangers of fanaticism and the thin line between love and madness.

- The True Knot (from *Doctor Sleep* by Stephen King): This group of quasi-immortal beings who feed off the "steam" of children with psychic powers is a modern take on the vampire mythos, representing parasitic exploitation and the fear of aging.

These characters, with their depth, flaws, and complexities, have left an indelible mark on horror literature. They serve as testament to the genre's ability to explore the human condition in its darkest shades. Through their tales, authors have not only entertained but have also probed deep philosophical and societal questions, making these characters timeless in their appeal and relevance. Can you write similar summaries for your characters?

Characters are the heartbeats of your story. Give them life, and they will breathe soul into your pages.

Understanding Archetypes and Nuances

In the world of storytelling, characters are like friends guiding us through their adventures. They're the heart and soul of a story, making us laugh, cry, and sometimes hide under the covers. Over time, we've seen certain types of characters pop up again and again, each with their own special flavor. Let's take stroll through some of these character types to see what makes them tick.

- The Hero: Think of the hero as the star quarterback of the story. They're usually fighting for good, standing up to the bad guys, and showing us what bravery looks like. But heroes aren't always perfect—sometimes they're a bit rough around the edges, which makes them feel more like real people.

- The Anti-Hero: This is the hero's rebellious cousin. They might not have the shiny armor or the perfect smile, but they've got grit. They're the ones who might bend the rules a bit, but deep down, they've got a heart of gold.

- The Fallen Hero: Picture a hero who took a wrong turn. They started off with all the right intentions but ended up on the dark side. Their story is a bit sad, showing us how even the best can lose their way.

- The Redeemed Villain: Everyone loves a good comeback story, right? This character starts off as the bad guy but ends up turning things around. It's like watching the school bully become the class president. It gives us hope that people can change for the better.

- The Mentor: Think of the wise old teacher who's seen it all. They're the ones dishing out advice and helping our hero get through tough times. They're like the guiding light in the dark forest of the story. Forgive me for using Dr. Cox from the show Scrubs as my favorite example.

- The Sidekick: Every hero needs a buddy. The sidekick is there to crack jokes, lend a hand, and sometimes get into a bit of trouble. They're the peanut butter to the hero's jelly.

- The Love Interest: Not just there for a smooch, the love interest has their own dreams and challenges. They're not just arm candy; they're a key part of the story, pushing the hero to be better or sometimes making them question everything.

- The Foil: This character is like the hero's mirror image, but a bit twisted. They show us what the hero could become if they're not careful. It's like looking at the hero through a funhouse mirror.

- The Trickster: Always up for a laugh or a prank, the trickster keeps things interesting. They remind us not to take life too seriously and to expect the unexpected.

- The Shapeshifter: Mysterious and hard to pin down, the shapeshifter keeps us guessing. Are they a friend or a foe? Their unpredictability adds a dash of mystery to the story.

These characters are the spices that make the story stew delicious. They bring different flavors, making the tale more exciting, emotional, and memorable. Whether they're heroes, villains, or something in between, each one adds a unique touch to the storytelling tapestry. So, next time you dive into a story, see if you can spot these familiar faces and enjoy the rich tapestry they weave.

Chapter 2

Crafting Authentic Characters

In the intricate tapestry of storytelling, characters are the vibrant threads that bring the narrative to life. For a story to truly resonate with its audience, it's crucial that these characters act and react in ways that are authentic to their established personalities, backgrounds, and motivations. When characters behave inconsistently, merely serving the plot's needs, it can disrupt the reader's immersion and diminish the story's impact. As an author, you need to ensure your characters remain true to themselves, while also acknowledging the complexities and unpredictability of human behavior. Some of this will sound a bit repetitive, but bear with me. It'll be worth it. Eventually you'll do all these things naturally, without feeling overwhelmed.

Motivation

Every action or reaction should stem from the character's internal motivations. If a character's decision seems out of sync with their personality or backstory, it's worth a second look.

However, it's important to recognize that characters, much like real people, can act out of character due to various factors. These deviations can add depth and realism to a story.

Here's how authors can effectively weave in such complexities:

- **Emotional Residue from Previous Scenes**
  Emotions don't reset at the end of a scene. If a character has faced something traumatic or exhilarating, those feelings can color their subsequent actions. An ordinarily patient character might be short-tempered after a distressing event.

- **Misunderstandings and Misinformation**
  In the realm of storytelling, the concept of characters acting on false beliefs presents a fascinating dynamic. This narrative device involves characters making decisions based on misunderstandings or misinformation, leading to actions that might appear out of character at first glance. However, these actions are perfectly aligned with the character's perception of their situation, offering a rich layer of complexity and realism to the story.

  When a character acts on a false belief, it reveals their vulnerabilities, biases, and the limits of their knowledge. It's a humanizing element, showing that characters, like real people, are susceptible to errors in judgment and can be misled or misinformed. This can stem from a variety of sources—a deceptive character, a misinterpreted event, or a flawed understanding of a critical piece of information. You'll find perfect examples of this in the Breaking Bad series.

  These actions based on false beliefs can drive the plot in unexpected directions, creating tension, conflict, and suspense. For the reader, there's the dramatic irony of knowing the truth while watching the character navigate through their misconception. This can lead to moments of frustration, empathy, or anticipation as the reader awaits the character's realization of their error.

  Furthermore, the moment of revelation, when the character discovers their belief is false, is often a pivotal point in the story. It can lead to a range of emotional responses—shock, embarrassment, guilt, or relief. This realization can be a catalyst for character development, forcing them to confront their flaws and biases, and in some cases, leading to a significant change in their trajectory.

- **External Manipulation**

External manipulation in storytelling is a powerful tool that can lead characters to act in ways that contradict their inherent nature. This manipulation can come from various sources—a cunning antagonist, societal pressures, lovers, or even close allies. When characters are coerced or manipulated, it often results in them making choices that they wouldn't normally consider, creating a fertile ground for internal conflict and moral dilemmas.

These situations force characters to confront their core values and priorities, challenging them to either stand firm or compromise their principles. It can lead to a deep exploration of their character, revealing hidden strengths or exposing underlying weaknesses. The internal struggle that ensues from such manipulation is compelling, as it showcases the character grappling with difficult choices, often under considerable pressure. This not only adds depth to the character but also drives the narrative forward, keeping readers engaged as they anticipate the outcomes of these conflicts.

- **Mood-Driven Decisions**

Mood-driven decisions in storytelling highlight the human tendency to act impulsively under the influence of intense emotions. Characters overwhelmed by feelings like anger, fear, joy, or despair may make snap decisions that deviate from their usual behavior. These moments are crucial, as they provide a glimpse into the character's raw, unguarded self, revealing vulnerabilities and strengths that are not evident in calmer times.

After the emotional tide recedes, characters often face the consequences of their impulsive actions. This period of reflection is a critical point in their development. It can lead to self-awareness, regret, or a reaffirmation of their beliefs and values. These sequences are not merely plot devices; they are pivotal moments that can set the course for a character's future actions and growth. They add a layer of realism and depth to the narrative, as readers witness the characters grappling with the fallout of their mood-driven choices, navigating the complexities of their emotions and the impact of their actions on themselves and others.

- **Growth and Change**

  Characters in a story are dynamic, evolving entities. Their growth and change are pivotal to the narrative, reflecting how experiences and interactions shape them over time. This evolution can manifest in various ways, influencing their actions and decisions. A character's journey might lead them to develop new perspectives, alter their beliefs, or adopt different behaviors. These changes, while potentially contrasting with their initial portrayal, align with their developmental arc.

  As characters navigate through the plot, they encounter situations that challenge their existing worldview, prompting them to adapt and grow. This transformation is a natural progression of their character arc, making their actions, even when seemingly divergent from their original nature, consistent with their evolving self. Such growth adds depth to the narrative, making characters more relatable and realistic, as it mirrors the continuous evolution of human beings in real life.

- **Contextual Behavior**

  Characters, much like real people, exhibit different facets of their personality in various settings, a concept known as contextual behavior. This multifaceted nature is crucial in creating depth and realism in characters. For instance, a character might display assertiveness in their professional life, taking charge in high-stress situations at work. However, in their personal life, they could be more reserved, perhaps overshadowed by more dominant family members or choosing to keep their opinions to themselves in social settings.

This variance in behavior across different contexts adds layers to a character's personality, showcasing their adaptability and the complexity of human nature. It also provides opportunities for conflict and growth, as characters navigate through these different environments, sometimes struggling to reconcile these varying aspects of their identity.

Contextual behavior can also be used to reveal hidden traits or secrets. A character who is typically gentle and kind might exhibit surprising aggression in a specific situation, hinting at a past trauma or a side of their personality that they keep hidden. By exploring how characters behave in different settings, authors can create more nuanced, believable characters that resonate with readers, reflecting the diverse ways in which people present themselves in various aspects of their lives.

- **Reactions to Stress or Trauma**
  In high-stress or traumatic situations, characters often display primal reactions such as fight, flight, or freeze responses. These instinctive behaviors can significantly enhance the authenticity of high-stakes scenes, revealing aspects of a character's personality that are not evident in normal circumstances. For example, a character who typically exhibits calm and collected behavior might unexpectedly choose to fight in a dangerous situation, showcasing a hidden reservoir of courage or desperation. Alternatively, a character known for their bravery might experience a freeze response, highlighting the overwhelming nature of a particular trauma or the complexity of human

psychology under extreme stress.

These reactions can also serve as pivotal moments in a character's development, marking a turning point in their narrative arc. The way a character responds to stress or trauma can lead to self-discovery, change their path, or affect their relationships with other characters. It's important for these reactions to feel genuine and consistent with the character's background and experiences, even if they seem surprising in the moment. By thoughtfully incorporating fight, flight, or freeze responses, authors can create more dynamic and compelling narratives, deepening the reader's engagement with the characters and the story. We'll dive deeper into this later on.

Wrapping it all up, keeping a character true to themselves is vital, but it's just as crucial to show how the world around them can shake things up. When writers mix in all the outside stuff that can affect what a character does—like the situations they find themselves in or the people they interact with—they end up with characters who feel real. These characters are unpredictable and deep, just like real people. This makes stories way more interesting and something readers can truly connect with.

Think of it like this: characters should be as complicated as real life. Our actions and how we react come from a mix of what's inside us and what's happening around us, including our feelings and what we've been through. When characters in a story have this kind of depth, the whole story feels more genuine and it pulls readers in deeper. It's not just about what the characters do, but why they do it.

"Don't be 'a writer.' Be writing."—**William Faulkner**

Avoid Plot-Driven Decisions

In crafting compelling narratives, one of the key aspects to consider is the balance between plot-driven and character-driven storytelling. While plot is undoubtedly important, it's the characters and their decisions that should ideally drive the narrative forward. This approach not only makes the story more relatable and engaging but also allows for more organic and unexpected developments.

Character-driven narratives focus on the decisions, emotions, and personal growth of the characters. Each choice a character makes should stem from their personality, background, and the situation they are in, rather than serving a pre-determined plot point. This approach ensures that the story unfolds in a way that feels natural and believable. For instance, a character's decision to confront a fear or challenge should be motivated by their personal journey and experiences, not just because the plot requires it.

When characters are the driving force behind the story, the plot evolves in a more organic manner. This can lead to unexpected twists and turns that are more surprising and satisfying for the reader. It also allows for deeper exploration of themes and ideas, as the narrative is shaped by the characters' diverse perspectives and reactions to events.

Character-driven stories often feature conflicts that are deeply personal and emotionally resonant. These conflicts arise naturally from the characters' desires, fears, and relationships, making them more impactful. For example, a conflict between two characters over a moral dilemma will be more engaging if it stems from their individual beliefs and past experiences, rather than being imposed by the needs of the plot.

Allowing characters to drive the narrative also provides flexibility in storytelling. As characters grow and change, the story can adapt and evolve in response to these developments. This dynamic approach keeps the narrative fresh and prevents it from becoming predictable or formulaic.

While character-driven narratives can be more challenging to write, as they require a deep understanding of each character, the rewards are significant. These stories tend to be more immersive and emotionally engaging, creating a stronger connection between the reader and the characters. They also offer more opportunities for character development and thematic exploration, enriching the overall reading experience.

In conclusion, avoiding plot-driven decisions in favor of character-driven narratives can lead to richer, more nuanced storytelling. By focusing on the characters and their choices, authors can create stories that resonate deeply with readers, offering unexpected twists and profound emotional impact.

Creating Unforgettable Minor Characters

In the world of storytelling, it's not just the heroes and villains who capture our hearts. Often, it's the smaller, side characters who leave a lasting impression, especially when their stories end too soon. The loss of a minor character can be a powerful moment in a story, stirring deep emotions and moving the plot along. Here's a guide on how authors can make these characters memorable and use their departure to deepen the narrative:

Making a Strong First Impression:
- Memorable Introductions: Even with limited time in the spotlight, make sure these characters stand out. It could be through a quirky trait, a meaningful moment, or an important interaction with a main character.

Adding Depth in Small Doses:
- Hints of a Backstory: Give glimpses into their past, hopes, or regrets.

These don't need to be elaborate but should add color to their character.

- Unique Voice: Make their dialogue stand out. This could be through a special way of talking, a catchphrase, or a unique perspective.

Building Connections:
- Relationships with Main Characters: Define their relationship with the main cast. This could range from a mentor-student bond to a deep friendship or a fleeting but impactful encounter.

- Memorable Moments: Craft scenes where they share insights, vulnerabilities, or joy with the main characters, making their eventual loss hit harder.

Playing a Key Role:
- Crucial to the Plot: They should contribute something vital to the story, whether it's crucial information, a sacrifice, or introducing a moral question.

Foreshadowing Their Fate:
- Subtle Clues: Drop hints about what's to come. This builds suspense and gets readers more attached, hoping they might somehow make it through.

The Impact of Their Departure:
- Emotional Resonance: Their exit should be significant. It needs to challenge the main characters, shift the plot, or highlight a key theme.

- A Fitting Tribute: Let other characters, and through them the readers, grieve and honor them. This closure underlines their influence and loss.

Leaving a Lasting Legacy:
- Ongoing Influence: Their absence should continue to affect the story and the protagonists, whether it's motivating them, changing their views, or presenting new obstacles.

- Keeping Their Memory Alive: Use references, flashbacks, or keepsakes to keep their memory woven into the story.

In short, the loss of a minor character can be a deeply impactful part of a story, but only if they're crafted with care and depth. By making readers care for them, even briefly, their loss becomes a moment of true emotional depth, adding layers of feeling, conflict, and richness to the narrative. It shows that in fiction, it's the depth of a character's journey, not its length, that really counts.

Crafting the Quintessential Villain

In the intricate ballet of storytelling, the hero and the villain are eternal dance partners, their movements and motivations intertwined in a delicate balance. While much emphasis is placed on crafting a relatable and compelling hero, the villain's role is equally, if not more, pivotal. A well-crafted villain can elevate a story, adding layers of tension, intrigue, and depth. So, how does one go about creating a villain worthy of their hero? Let's delve into the dark arts of villain creation.

- Understand Their Motivations: Every villain believes they are the hero of their own story. They don't wake up deciding to be evil for the sake of being evil. Whether it's a thirst for power, a quest for revenge, or a twisted sense of justice, a villain's motivations drive their actions. Dive deep into their psyche, understand their desires, fears, and the events that shaped them. This not only makes them more believable but also more relatable. A favorite of mine is Wilson Fisk in Daredevil.

- Make Them Complex: Stereotypical, one-dimensional villains are forgettable. The most memorable villains are those with depth and complexity. Perhaps they show moments of vulnerability or have a tragic backstory that led them down a dark path. Maybe they occasionally display kindness or have a code of honor they won't break. These nuances make them unpredictable and more human, adding layers to their character.

- A Worthy Adversary: A villain should challenge the hero, pushing them to their limits. They should be formidable, possessing skills, intelligence, or resources that make them a genuine threat. This creates tension and stakes, making the hero's journey more perilous and the eventual confrontation more anticipated.

- Reflect or Contrast the Hero: As mentioned before, a great villain can mirror the hero's qualities or stand in stark contrast to them. If your hero is a beacon of hope and morality, a nihilistic villain who believes in the futility of existence can be a compelling antagonist. Alternatively, a villain who shares similar traits or background with the hero but made different choices can create a fascinating dynamic, making the hero question their own path.

- Evolve with the Story: Just as heroes grow and evolve, so should the villain. As the narrative progresses, reveal more about the villain—their past, their vulnerabilities, their evolving plans. This keeps the readers engaged and invested in their journey, even if they don't agree with their methods.

- Avoid Overused Tropes: While certain villainous tropes are popular, relying too heavily on them can make your antagonist feel clichéd. Examples include The Evil Genius, The Vengeful Ex, The Mad Scientist, and the Femme Fatale. Challenge yourself to subvert these tropes or approach them from a fresh angle.

- Personal Connection: A personal connection between the hero and the villain adds emotional depth to their conflict. Whether they share a past, have mutual loved ones, or their destinies are intertwined, this connection makes their confrontations more than just physical battles; they become emotional and ideological clashes.

Crafting a compelling villain is a nuanced process that requires understanding, empathy, and a touch of darkness. By ensuring they are multi-dimensional, motivated, and deeply intertwined with the hero's journey, you create not just an antagonist, but a character that readers will remember long after the story ends. In the dance of hero and villain, make sure your villain leads just as often as they follow, creating a narrative tango that captivates your audience.

> Crafting characters is like sculpting shadows—we give form to fears, hopes, and dreams, breathing life into the very heart of our stories.

Mining for Characters: Unearthing Inspiration from the World Around

For authors, the world is a treasure trove of inspiration, teeming with potential characters waiting to be discovered and brought to life on the page. But where exactly should one look?

I've always believed in the power of real-world inspiration for character creation. To help out authors on Crystal Lake Entertainment's Patreon, I've recommended on many occasions that authors step outside their usual environments and routines, to observe the world around them with fresh eyes. I urge them to go out into the world, to look at strangers not just as passersby but as potential characters, rich with stories and nuances waiting to be explored.

Eavesdropping on conversations, for instance, can be a goldmine. Overheard snippets of dialogue at a café or in a park can spark ideas for a character's background, personality, or current dilemma. It's not just about the words spoken, but the way they're said—the pauses, the laughter, the sighs—all these elements breathe life into characters.

These real-world explorations are more than just exercises; they're adventures in human observation and empathy. By immersively engaging with the world around us, we can find inspiration in the most unexpected places and people. From the old man feeding pigeons with a story etched in every wrinkle to the young woman passionately arguing on the phone, every individual holds a universe within them, ripe for exploration in our stories.

So, as we delve into the various sources of character inspiration, remember that the world around us is vibrant with potential muses. It's our task as storytellers to notice them, understand them, and transform them into compelling characters that resonate with our readers.

1. Personal Experiences and Memories:

When it comes to crafting memorable characters in fiction, one of the richest sources of inspiration can be found in our own personal experiences and memories. The people we meet, the emotions we feel, and the experiences we undergo all contribute to a wellspring of material that can breathe life into the characters we create.

Often, the most memorable and authentic characters are those inspired by real people we've encountered in our lives. These could be individuals we've met briefly but who left a lasting impression, or those we've known for years, observing their quirks, habits, and perspectives. Think about someone who caught your attention in a crowd, or a friend whose life story always fascinated you. What was it about them that stood out? Perhaps it was a distinctive mannerism, a unique way of speaking, or an unusual outlook on life. These real-life encounters provide a wealth of material for creating characters that are vivid, believable, and compelling.

Beyond just external observations, tapping into our own personal emotions and experiences can add depth and authenticity to our characters. As authors, we have a treasure trove of feelings and memories to draw from. Reflect on the emotions you've felt during pivotal moments in your life—joy, sorrow, fear, love, anger, or surprise. Consider how these emotions influenced your actions and decisions. By channeling these feelings into your characters, you can create individuals who are not just figments of imagination but reflections of real human experiences. Be sure to check out later chapters on mental health. Many authors have fallen victim to depression, since it's our job to open ourselves to emotions and not block out said pivotal moments.

Think about a time when you felt extreme joy or profound sadness. How did your body react? What were your thoughts? How did you interact with others? These introspections can help you craft characters who respond to situations in ways that readers can relate to and empathize with. It's not just about replicating the exact experience, but about capturing the essence of the emotion and translating it into your character's context.

Moreover, drawing from personal experiences can help in creating characters with a rich backstory. Every person has a history, a series of events and choices that have shaped who they are. As an author, you can delve into your own past or imagine the past of someone you know to build a character's history. This backstory will inform how they act and react in the narrative, making them more rounded and believable.

Incorporating personal experiences and emotions into character creation also allows for a more intimate connection between the author and the story. It can be a cathartic process, where you explore and make sense of your own experiences through the lens of your characters. This not only enriches the character but also adds a layer of authenticity to the narrative.

2. History and Biographies:

In the journey of becoming a masterful author, especially in the realm of horror, an intimate knowledge of history and the lives of those who have shaped it is invaluable. History, with its rich tapestry of events, personalities, and transformations, offers a deep well of inspiration for character creation. Historical figures, with their complex lives, monumental challenges, and often enigmatic personalities, can serve as a goldmine for crafting compelling characters in fiction.

Reading a few biographies and historical accounts can (will) provide a window into the motivations, strengths, and flaws of real-life individuals. These narratives offer more than just facts; they delve into the psychological and emotional landscapes of historical figures, revealing the human side of history. For a horror author, this is particularly potent. The genre often explores the darker aspects of human nature and the macabre elements of our past. Understanding the motivations behind historical figures' actions, especially those involved in darker chapters of history, can provide a rich background for creating nuanced, multi-dimensional characters.

History is full of stories of conflict, survival, betrayal, and redemption—themes that are central to horror fiction. By studying how real people navigated these challenges, authors can gain insights into human resilience, the capacity for evil, and the complexity of moral choices. These insights can then be woven into fictional characters, making them more realistic and relatable.

Similarly, the lives of ordinary people in extraordinary circumstances—such as war, plague, or social upheaval—can inspire characters who are resilient, resourceful, and complex.

By drawing from the vast reservoir of human history, authors can craft stories that are not only terrifying but also richly woven with the threads of reality, making them all the more haunting and unforgettable.

3. Travel and Cultural Exploration:

Experiencing new cultures, customs, and lifestyles can offer a plethora of character ideas. The way people live, their traditions, beliefs, and daily challenges can provide a rich backdrop for character development.

- Diverse Perspectives: Travel exposes you to a variety of perspectives. You encounter people whose life experiences, beliefs, and values differ vastly from your own. This exposure broadens your understanding of human nature, allowing you to create characters with depth and authenticity.

- Cultural Nuances: Every culture has its unique nuances, from language and customs to social norms and values. As an author, observing these subtleties can help you craft characters that truly embody the essence of these cultures, making them more than just stereotypes.

- Real-Life Inspirations: Meeting people from different walks of life can inspire characters who are complex and multifaceted. A conversation with a local artisan, a shared meal with a family, or observing the daily hustle of city life can all spark ideas for characters with rich backstories and motivations.

- Sensory Experiences: Travel engages all your senses. The sights, sounds, smells, and textures of new places can be woven into your narrative, bringing your characters and their settings to life. A character's reaction to a bustling market, a serene landscape, or a crowded city street can reveal much about their personality and background.

- Challenging Preconceptions: Being in unfamiliar settings challenges your preconceptions and biases. This personal growth reflects in your writing, enabling you to create characters who are not just reflections of your own experiences but are shaped by a broader understanding of the world.

- Emotional Connections: Travel often evokes strong emotions—awe, curiosity, loneliness, joy, or even frustration. These emotions can be channeled into your characters, making their experiences more relatable and compelling.

- Storytelling Traditions: Different cultures have their unique storytelling traditions. Learning about these can inspire new ways of developing characters and their arcs, adding a fresh twist to familiar tropes.

Travel and cultural exploration are not just about seeing new places; they're about experiencing life through different lenses. As an author, these experiences are invaluable. They enrich your understanding of the human condition, allowing you to create characters that resonate with readers from all walks of life. Whether it's through the eyes of a character exploring their own culture or stepping into an entirely new world, these journeys can transform the way you approach character development in your writing.

4. Literature and Media:
Literature and media are invaluable resources for authors in the realm of character creation. They provide a wide range of examples and styles, from the intricacies of human behavior in classic literature to the dynamic character portrayals in modern media. By engaging with these sources, you can expand

your understanding of character development, enriching your own writing with well-rounded, compelling characters that captivate your readers.

- Classic Literature: Classics are treasure troves of character study. From the tragic heroes of Shakespeare to the complex figures in Tolstoy's novels, these works offer insights into human nature and the societal norms of their times. Studying these characters can help you understand how to create timeless characters that resonate across ages.

- Contemporary Novels: Modern literature reflects current societal issues and diverse perspectives. Exploring characters from contemporary novels can provide ideas on how to write characters that are relevant to today's readers, dealing with modern dilemmas and complexities.

- Non-Fiction: As mentioned before, biographies, memoirs, and historical texts introduce real-life characters with rich, layered stories. These accounts can inspire you to create characters based on real human experiences, lending authenticity and depth to your narrative.

- Movies and TV Shows: Visual Character Studies
  - Visual media allows you to study character development in a dynamic way. Observing a character's body language, facial expressions, and interactions adds another layer to understanding character construction.
  - Movies and TV shows often have well-defined character arcs. Analyzing how characters evolve over time, how they handle conflicts, and their journey can provide valuable insights for developing your characters' arcs. I'd actually suggest mapping the ARC from one of your favorite series characters as an exercise.
  - Different genres—from drama to science fiction—showcase a wide range of character types. Exploring various genres can help you understand how to adapt character traits to fit different narrative styles and settings.

- The way characters speak and interact with each other in films and shows is a great study in dialogue writing. Observing these interactions can improve your ability to write realistic and engaging dialogues.
- Sometimes, the visual representation of a character can spark inspiration. The way a character is dressed, their mannerisms, or even the setting they are in can give you ideas for creating vivid, memorable characters.

5. Art and Photography:
Art and photography are not just visual treats. They are powerful catalysts for the imagination, especially for authors in search of character inspiration. The subjects captured in these mediums can serve as the foundation for rich, multi-dimensional characters in your writing.

- When you study a portrait, you're not just looking at a face; you're encountering a story. Each brushstroke can represent an aspect of the subject's life. What were their dreams, fears, or secrets? A painting of a stern-faced woman or a contemplative young man can be the starting point for a character's personality, background, and motivations.

- Sculptures, especially those depicting humans, are frozen moments in time. They can represent an emotion, a historical figure, or a mythical character. Observing the details in a sculpture—the posture, the expression, the attire—can inspire the creation of a character with depth and history.

- Candid photographs are snapshots of real life. They capture people in moments of joy, sorrow, or everyday life. A black-and-white photograph of a crowded street, a candid shot of a laughing child, or a solemn image of an elderly person—each tells a story. These images can prompt questions about the subjects' lives, leading to the development of characters with rich backstories and authentic emotions.

- Art and photography often leave room for interpretation. This ambiguity is a gift to authors, allowing you to weave narratives around what you perceive in an image. The subject's expression, the setting, the colors—all these elements can be interpreted in myriad ways, each leading to a different character story.

Art and photography offer a unique avenue for character inspiration. They challenge authors to look beyond the surface, to imagine the stories behind the faces and scenes captured in these mediums. By engaging with art and photography, you can enrich your character development process, creating characters that are as vivid and compelling as the images that inspired them.

6. Nature and Environment:
Nature and the environment are vast, untapped sources of inspiration for character creation, offering a diverse palette of elements that can shape and define the personalities and stories of your characters, especially for characters in horror fiction.

- The animal kingdom is replete with fascinating behaviors and traits that can be mirrored in human characters. For instance, the loyalty of a dog, the independence of a cat, or the cunning of a fox can be translated into human characteristics, giving rise to unique and memorable characters. Observing animals in their natural habitat or even as pets can provide insights into these traits. Shouldn't your villain have the characteristics of a predator?

- The setting in which a character is placed—whether it's the chaotic energy of a bustling city or the tranquil solitude of the countryside—can significantly influence their demeanor, aspirations, and life challenges. A character raised in a rural, isolated environment might have a different worldview compared to someone from an urban setting. These environmental influences can shape their motivations, their interactions with other characters, and their responses to various situations.

- Nature also serves as a rich source of metaphors that can be used to deepen character development. The resilience of a tree standing tall through storms, the adaptability of a river carving its path, or the transformation of a caterpillar into a butterfly—these natural phenomena can be symbolic of a character's journey or traits. We've certainly read many similar character ARCs.

- The sensory experiences offered by different environments—the sounds, smells, and sights—can also be integrated into a character's development. How a character reacts to the scent of rain, the sound of waves crashing, or the sight of a bustling market can reveal subtle nuances of their personality and background.

Nature and the environment are not just backdrops for storytelling; they are active participants in character development. By observing and integrating elements from the natural world and different environments, authors can create characters that are not only relatable and authentic but also reflective of the diverse and intricate world we live in.

7. Dreams and Daydreams:
Dreams and daydreams are like uncharted territories of our subconscious, brimming with creative potential for character creation. These mental escapades often weave together the most unexpected elements, presenting characters, scenarios, and emotions that, while surreal, can be incredibly compelling when adapted into fiction.

- Dreams are the subconscious mind's way of telling stories, often bringing forth characters and narratives that we might not consciously think of. These dream-born characters can be bizarre, enigmatic, or strikingly vivid, offering a fresh perspective or inspiration for a story.

- Dreams often evoke strong emotions, whether it's fear, joy, sadness, or something more abstract. These emotions can be a powerful tool in character development, providing a deeper understanding of a character's psychological landscape.

- The surreal and often illogical nature of dreams can lead to unique character traits or backgrounds. A character inspired by a dream might have an unconventional worldview, mysterious abilities, or an intriguing backstory that sets them apart from typical character archetypes.

Tapping into our dreams and daydreams can unlock a treasure trove of character ideas, imbued with emotional depth and a touch of the surreal, enriching our stories with characters that resonate with readers on a subconscious level.

8. People-Watching:

People-watching is an intriguing and often underutilized tool for authors, especially in the realm of horror fiction. As mentioned before, it's a favorite recommendation of mine. By sitting quietly in a café, park, or bustling train station, you can observe the myriad of characters that pass by. Each person carries a unique story, a set of relationships, hidden secrets, and unspoken aspirations. As a horror writer, you can delve deeper, imagining not just their everyday lives but also their fears, the skeletons in their closets, or the dark secrets they might harbor. This exercise not only sparks creativity but also helps in building complex, multi-dimensional characters that can add depth and realism to your horror narratives. Be prepared. We'll definitely mention this again when we talk about creating amazing dialogue.

9. Personal Challenges and Philosophies:

Drawing from your own beliefs, moral dilemmas, and personal challenges can be a profound source of inspiration for character development in horror writing. By projecting aspects of your own life philosophy, ethical quandaries, and the obstacles you've faced onto a character, you create a multi-dimensional individual who resonates with authenticity. This approach allows you to explore deeper, often darker aspects of human nature and psychology, which is a cornerstone of effective horror storytelling. Characters grappling with issues that are personally significant to you can lead to more passionate and compelling narratives, as they navigate a world filled with fear, uncertainty, and the macabre, mirroring your own internal struggles and reflections.

10. Mythology and Folklore:

Mythology and folklore are treasure troves of character inspiration, especially for horror fiction. These ancient narratives are rich with heroes, anti-heroes, gods, monsters, and mortals, each embodying timeless human fears, desires, and moral complexities. By delving into these age-old stories, you can unearth a plethora of character archetypes and narratives that have captivated human imagination for centuries.

Reimagining these characters for contemporary narratives allows you to bridge the gap between the ancient and the modern, creating a unique blend of horror that resonates with both historical depth and present-day relevance. For instance, a mythological creature can be reinterpreted to symbolize modern-day anxieties, or a legendary hero's journey can be adapted to explore contemporary moral dilemmas.

This approach not only enriches your story with a sense of timelessness but also provides a familiar framework for readers, making the horror elements more impactful. By drawing on mythology and folklore, you tap into the collective unconscious, leveraging archetypes and narratives that have shaped human

113

storytelling, and infusing them with a fresh, often terrifying, perspective. This fusion of the old and the new in horror writing can lead to stories that are both deeply rooted in tradition and strikingly relevant to today's readers.

Inspiration for characters is everywhere, waiting to be noticed and nurtured. By remaining curious, observant, and open-minded, authors can find a myriad of characters hidden in the world's nooks and crannies, just waiting to leap onto the page.

> "Always ask yourself, 'How can I enrich my readers' lives?' Whether through your stories or unexpected acts of kindness, make your readers' joy your priority."

Free Will: A Cheesy but Effective Practice for Character Development
by Chad Lutzke

I love sharing the genesis of creation when it comes to something I've written—if someone asks how I came up with the idea for a book, or who one particular character is based on, or giving some behind-the-scenes info on a standout scene. Suddenly I'm in the position to tell a story within a story, like when asked about my novel *Skullface Boy*, where a deformed young man goes on a hitchhiking road trip. I get to share that the entire book was mapped out on Google traffic view as I wrote it, using real locations as prompts for what happens to the protagonist in each chapter.

But when it comes to the actual creation of a character, I don't have much to offer. With the exception of the characters in my Jex series of books (*The Same Deep Water as You* and its prequels), who are all based on real people, I've got nothing interesting to say about the birth of any character because they're created in the spur of the moment, though I can offer this: Before I started writing seriously, I thought it was cheesy when I'd hear an author say things like, "The characters took over" or "I just go where the characters take me," as if the author wasn't responsible for their own words.

Years later, it still sounds cheesy. But I get it. It kind of does happen like that. The words do seem to have a life of their own. Each sentence built is the spark for another idea, every line a building block to further the story, and oftentimes those sparks cause a fire that's uncontrollable, turning the book you thought you had planned in your head into something else. For me, by the time I'm done, it's difficult to recall how my characters were created. Sparks fly, and the fire starts. That's it really, with nearly everything I've written. I allowed the characters their own free will.

A perfect example of a character that took on a life of his own is Roddy from *The Neon Owl*. Originally Roddy was to be nothing more than a drunk with one leg who stumbles into the apartment office and causes a scene. But I enjoyed Roddy's company. He was funny. I knew deep down he was a good guy. We just happened to catch him at a bad time. Before I knew it, I found out that despite being in his sixties, this was the first time Roddy had ever been drunk. I started having empathy for this one-legged handyman who loves ranch dressing. A man who sleeps with an elderly call girl to fill the void left by his wife—who he believes was killed by Ted Bundy in the seventies.

I'm not the only one who fell in love with Roddy. He happens to be everyone's favorite character in the book. Based on emails I've received and reviews I've read, people want more of him. He's the real star.

I'm so glad I gave him that free will, and as cheesy as it sounds, let him have a life of his own.

I suppose I can offer you the obvious advice and tell you to base your characters on people you've met. Frankenstein them. Take the mannerisms of Joe Blow down the street and fuse it with the stride of your mailman and the temperament of your mother-in-law, maybe give him your dog's eyes and your own ideals, but I think those things tend to come out on a subconscious level anyway. Instead, focus on letting them create themselves. If you don't like them, there's always the delete button.

Character Flaws and Strengths: Crafting the Multifaceted Human Experience

Characters, much like real people, are a blend of strengths and flaws. This intricate balance is what makes them relatable, compelling, and memorable. While strengths can make a character admirable, it's often their flaws that make them human, vulnerable, and genuine. Let's explore the art of crafting characters with a harmonious blend of strengths and flaws, ensuring they resonate with depth and authenticity.

1. The Role of Strengths:

- A character's strengths are pivotal in driving the plot of a story. These attributes enable them to confront and surmount various obstacles, make critical decisions that shape the course of the narrative, and exert influence over other characters and events. Their strengths, whether it be courage, intelligence, or charisma, become the catalysts for action and change, propelling the story forward and keeping readers engaged as they navigate the challenges and triumphs alongside the character.

- Characters' strengths, encompassing skills, moral values, or innate talents, play a crucial role in building rapport with readers. These positive traits endear the characters to the audience, fostering a connection that makes readers invested in their journeys. As readers recognize and admire these strengths, they find themselves rooting for the characters' successes and empathizing with their struggles, creating a deeper, more meaningful engagement with the story.

- Over the course of a narrative, characters often undergo significant evolution and growth. This development can manifest in the acquisition of new strengths or the refinement of existing ones. Such changes reflect the character's journey and personal evolution, illustrating how they adapt and grow in response to the challenges and experiences they encounter. This aspect of character development not only adds depth to the story but also resonates with readers, who often find inspiration in witnessing a character's growth and transformation.

2. The Significance of Flaws:

- Character flaws are pivotal in storytelling, fueling both internal and external conflicts. Internally, flaws like pride or fear lead to personal struggles and moral dilemmas. Externally, they cause misunderstandings and mistakes, impacting relationships and plot progression. These imperfections drive the story's tension and drama, making characters relatable and their journeys compelling. Flaws not only add depth to characters but also propel the narrative, creating suspense and engagement for the reader.

- Flaws in characters foster a sense of relatability and empathy among readers, which is extremely important in creating a page-turner. Everyone has imperfections, and seeing these reflected in a story's characters creates a deeper connection. This shared human experience, through the lens of a character's flaws, allows readers to see parts of themselves in the narrative, enhancing their emotional investment in the story. It's this reflection of real-life imperfections that makes characters more human and stories more engaging.

- Flaws in characters present opportunities for growth and transformation. Overcoming or coming to terms with personal imperfections often forms the heart of a character's journey. This evolution, whether it's learning from mistakes or accepting inherent weaknesses, adds depth to the narrative. It's through these struggles and eventual growth that characters become more layered and compelling, offering readers a satisfying arc of transformation and self-discovery.

3. Balancing the Two:

- Creating characters that resonate with readers often involves striking a balance between strengths and flaws. A character who appears too perfect can often feel unrealistic and distant, lacking the depth and relatability that come with imperfection. Introducing flaws is not just about adding a layer of vulnerability—it's about crafting a more believable and engaging persona. These flaws, whether they are insecurities, weaknesses, or moral shortcomings, make characters more human and relatable. They provide a window into the character's struggles, aspirations, and humanity, allowing readers to connect with them on a deeper level. By avoiding the trap of perfection, authors can create characters that are not only more realistic but also more compelling, as their vulnerabilities often drive the narrative forward, leading to growth, conflict, and ultimately, a more engaging story.

- Just as a flawless character can seem unrealistic, a character who embodies pure villainy without any redeeming qualities can also come across as one-dimensional. In crafting compelling antagonists, it's important to imbue them with shades of gray. These nuances add depth and complexity, making them more than just a foil to the protagonist. Even villains should have motivations, histories, or traits that humanize them, whether it's a tragic past, a noble goal gone awry, or moments of kindness and vulnerability. This approach not only makes the character more interesting and believable but also enriches the narrative. It invites readers to explore the complexities of good and evil, right and wrong, and to see the antagonist as a fully realized character rather than a mere obstacle for the hero. By steering clear of pure villainy, authors can create antagonists who are as layered and intriguing as their protagonists, and that's a vital ingredient for an amazing book.

4. Using Flaws and Strengths Together:

- The interplay between a character's strengths and flaws can significantly influence their decision-making process. For example, a character might possess the strength of high intelligence, which typically aids in problem-solving and strategic thinking. However, if this intelligence is coupled with the flaw of overthinking, it can lead to 'paralysis by analysis.' In such cases, the character's ability to process information deeply and thoroughly becomes a double-edged sword. While they can understand complex situations with remarkable clarity, their tendency to overanalyze can prevent them from making timely decisions. This dynamic creates a realistic and relatable conflict within the character, as they struggle to balance their intellectual prowess with the practical need to act. Such intricacies in a character's personality not only make them more engaging but also drive the plot in interesting and often unexpected directions. The push and pull between their strengths and weaknesses become a key factor in how events unfold, making their journey more compelling for the reader.

Don't let this intellectual dive into writing horror fiction overwhelm you and keep you from just sitting down and writing with creative freedom. Read the book, take what you need, and *just keep writing*.

- The dynamics of relationships in fiction are deeply influenced by the interplay of characters' strengths and flaws. A particular flaw in a character might be a source of irritation or conflict in one relationship, while the same trait could be endearing or complementary in another. For instance, a character's blunt honesty might strain their relationship with a sensitive friend who prefers gentle communication. However, this same trait of straightforwardness could be highly valued and even admired by another character who appreciates directness and despises pretense.

This complexity in relationships adds depth and realism to the narrative. It shows how different aspects of a character's personality can have varied impacts depending on the context and the people they interact with. Such nuances in character interactions not only enrich the story but also mirror the complexities of real-life relationships, where people respond differently to the same traits based on their own personalities, experiences, and expectations. By exploring these varied dynamics, authors can create a rich tapestry of interpersonal relationships that are both intriguing and relatable to readers.

5. Evolution Over Time:

- In the evolving journey of a character, the passage of time and the accumulation of experiences often lead to significant personal growth. As characters confront and navigate the consequences of their flaws, they gain insights and wisdom, allowing them to transform these weaknesses into strengths or develop effective coping mechanisms. How else can they defeat the monster at the end of the story? This evolution is further enriched as characters encounter new challenges. These situations often reveal hidden strengths, previously unknown or dormant, adding unexpected layers and dimensions to their persona. This process of learning from mistakes and adapting to new circumstances not only makes characters more complex and relatable but also mirrors the human experience of growth and adaptation in the face of life's ever-changing landscape.

Crafting characters is akin to painting a portrait. While bold strokes of strengths define the outline, it's the intricate details of flaws that add depth, shadow, and realism. As authors, your goal is to create characters that live and breathe on the page, reflecting the multifaceted nature of the human experience. By balancing strengths with flaws, you ensure our characters are not just figures in a story but reflections of real-life complexities, aspirations, and vulnerabilities. In the end, it's this balance that makes characters linger in readers' minds long after the last page is turned.

Chapter 3

Getting to Know Your Characters: The Author's Intimate Journey

In the vast tapestry of storytelling, characters are the threads that give color, texture, and depth to the narrative. They are the heartbeats that resonate with readers, making tales memorable and impactful. But for an author, the relationship with characters goes beyond mere creation; it's about understanding, intimacy, and depth. Here's why and how you should embark on the journey of truly getting to know your characters:

• The Iceberg Principle: Much like an iceberg, where 90% of its mass is hidden beneath the surface, a character's depth lies in the details not explicitly mentioned in the story. While readers might only see a fraction of the character's life, knowing their backstory, dreams, fears, and secrets can add layers to their personality, making them more authentic and relatable. And easier to write.

• Consistency is Key: By understanding your characters inside out, you ensure consistency in their actions, reactions, and decisions throughout the narrative. Even if certain details never make it to the page, they influence the character's choices, making them more believable.

• Fuel for Subtext: The unspoken details, the subtle hints, and the layers beneath the surface dialogue are all enriched when you, as the author, have a profound understanding of your characters. This depth provides the subtext, the unsaid emotions, and the underlying tensions that make scenes riveting. The more time your character spends in your mind, even when you're not writing, the more you'll find yourself thinking up scenarios or dilemmas for your character and book.

• Emotional Connection: The more you know about your characters, the more emotionally invested you become in their journeys. This emotional connection translates to the page, making readers equally invested in the characters' outcomes. It'll also motivate you through the difficult writing stages to come.

• Flexibility in Plotting: When you know your characters deeply, you can predict how they'd react in any given situation. This knowledge can be a boon when plotting, allowing for organic story developments based on character decisions rather than forced plot points.

How to Dive Deep into Your Characters

While the readers might only see the tip of the iceberg, it's the author's responsibility to understand the vastness beneath. By deeply knowing your characters, you not only enrich your narrative but also create authentic, memorable figures that resonate long after the story ends. Remember, in the world of fiction, characters are as real as the depth the author perceives in them.

Character Interviews:
Delving into the minds and hearts of your characters can be one of the most enriching aspects of writing. One effective way to achieve this is through character interviews. This technique involves sitting down and 'interviewing' your characters as if they were real people. Ask them about their past experiences, their aspirations, their deepest fears, and their most profound regrets. Inquire about their relationships, their views on the world, and the pivotal moments that shaped them.

By doing this, you allow your characters to reveal themselves to you beyond the confines of your plot. This process can uncover surprising details that enrich your narrative and provide a deeper understanding of their motivations and reactions. It's not just about their role in your story, but about who they are as individuals. These interviews can lead to more authentic and multi-dimensional characters, making your story more compelling and relatable. As you listen to their 'voices, you'll find that your characters become more than just fictional creations; they start to breathe and live on the page, adding a layer of realism and depth to your writing.

Write Unseen Scenes:
An intriguing way to add depth to your characters is to write unseen scenes from their lives. These are moments that have significantly impacted them but don't necessarily appear in your book. By crafting these scenes, you delve into their past, exploring pivotal experiences that have shaped their personalities, fears, and desires.

This exercise is akin to an archeological dig into your characters' histories. You might write about a defining incident in their childhood, a lost love, a moment of failure or triumph, or a painful goodbye. These scenes can reveal why a character is afraid of commitment, why they react strongly to certain situations, or why they hold specific beliefs.

By understanding these unseen moments, you gain a richer perspective on your characters' motivations and reactions within the main narrative. It's like piecing together a jigsaw puzzle of their psyche, where each hidden scene adds clarity and depth to the overall picture. This process not only enhances your understanding of your characters but also enriches the reader's experience, as the echoes of these unseen scenes subtly influence the character's actions and decisions in the story, making them more authentic and relatable.

Journaling:
Journaling from your character's perspective is a powerful tool for exploring their inner world. It involves writing diary entries as if you are the character, delving into their thoughts, feelings, and experiences. This exercise can cover a

typical day in their life, a cherished or traumatic memory, or their reflections on a pivotal event in your story.

Imagine sitting down with a pen and paper, or at a keyboard, and stepping into your character's shoes. What would they write about? What worries keep them up at night? What small joys do they cherish? Through this process, you can uncover layers of their personality that might not be evident in the main narrative.

A journal entry could reveal their deepest fears, unfulfilled desires, or hidden conflicts. It could provide insight into how they perceive other characters and events in the story. This exercise is particularly useful for understanding your character's voice and perspective, making them more three-dimensional and real. It's a chance to let them speak directly to you, without the constraints of the plot or other characters. By regularly journaling as your character, you can maintain a consistent and authentic voice for them throughout your writing, enhancing the reader's connection and empathy toward them.

Challenge Them:
Challenging your characters by placing them in situations outside the scope of your story is a dynamic way to explore and reveal hidden facets of their personality. This exercise involves imagining scenarios that are not part of your main narrative and considering how your character would react in these circumstances.

For instance, how would your character handle a crisis unrelated to the central plot? What if they were faced with a moral dilemma that tests their values in a way the story doesn't? Or, how would they react to an unexpected joy or an unforeseen tragedy? These hypothetical situations can be as mundane or as extraordinary as you like.

By observing how your character navigates these scenarios, you can gain insights into aspects of their personality that you hadn't considered before. It can reveal their strengths, weaknesses, fears, and desires. This exercise is particularly useful for developing a well-rounded character, ensuring they are not just reacting to the story's events but are proactive individuals with their own set of complex reactions and emotions.

Additionally, this method can help in creating a more consistent character. Understanding how they would react in various situations ensures that their actions within the story are in line with their established personality. It can also inspire new plot ideas or subplots that enrich the main narrative, making your story more engaging and your characters more relatable and memorable.

Mind Mapping:
Mind mapping is a creative and effective tool for authors to delve deeper into their characters' psyche, relationships, and journey. This technique involves creating a visual representation that connects various aspects of a character's life, such as their background, fears, dreams, relationships, and pivotal moments.

Start by placing your character's name in the center of a blank page. From there, draw branches that represent different aspects of their life. For instance, one branch could be dedicated to their family background, another to their deepest fears, and yet another to their aspirations and dreams. Further branches can explore their relationships with other characters, their role in the story, and key events that have shaped them.

Each branch can then be expanded with sub-branches, adding details and layers. For example, under 'fears,' you might add specific phobias or insecurities your character has, and under 'dreams,' you could list their goals and aspirations, both big and small. This process not only aids in fleshing out your character but also in understanding how different elements of their life interconnect and influence their actions and decisions in the story.

Mind mapping is particularly useful for visual thinkers, as it allows you to see the relationships between different aspects of your character's life at a glance. It can also be a dynamic tool for brainstorming and generating new ideas for character development and plot progression.

As you build your mind map, you might discover new connections or aspects of your character that you hadn't considered before. This can lead to more nuanced and layered character portrayal, making them more realistic and relatable to readers. Additionally, this visual representation can serve as a quick reference guide as you write, helping you maintain consistency in your character's actions and reactions throughout your story.

Reactions to Stress

In the crucible of conflict, characters are tested, their true natures laid bare. Stressful situations, whether they arise from external threats or internal dilemmas, act as catalysts, accelerating character development and revealing hidden facets of their personalities. How a character reacts under pressure can be one of the most telling aspects of their persona, offering readers insights into their core traits, vulnerabilities, and potential for growth. Let's explore the significance of characters' reactions to stress and how they shape narrative arcs.

1. The Revealing Nature of Crisis:
In the crucible of crisis, characters often reveal their true selves, stripped of the masks they wear in times of calm. These high-stress moments can unmask hidden facets of their personalities, offering glimpses into their genuine nature. While some characters may respond in ways that align with their established traits, others might react unexpectedly, surprising readers and hinting at previously concealed depths or unresolved past traumas. Such reactions not only deepen character development but also add a layer of unpredictability and intrigue to the narrative.

2. Types of Stress Reactions:
Stress can trigger a spectrum of primal reactions in characters, ranging from the instinctual fight, flight, or freeze responses to more nuanced emotional

outbursts. Characters might confront challenges head-on, aggressively tackling obstacles, or they could choose avoidance, retreating into denial or inaction. Alternatively, they might freeze, paralyzed by the situation at hand. Additionally, stress can heighten emotions, leading to varied responses like tears, anger, laughter, or a seemingly stoic, controlled demeanor. These varied reactions not only reflect a character's personality but also add depth and realism to their portrayal in stressful situations.

3. The Role of Backstory:
The role of a character's backstory is pivotal in shaping their reactions to stress. Characters with traumatic pasts often display heightened or altered responses to stressful situations. For instance, a character who has experienced abandonment might react with panic in scenarios where they feel left behind or isolated. Additionally, stress responses can be influenced by learned behaviors, which are deeply ingrained and shaped by factors such as upbringing, cultural background, or significant past experiences. These elements of a character's history play a crucial role in determining how they handle stress, adding layers of complexity and authenticity to their reactions in the narrative.

4. Growth Through Adversity:
Growth through adversity is a crucial theme in character development, particularly in how characters respond to stress. The process of learning from and adapting to stressful situations can significantly chart a character's growth trajectory. Characters may initially react in maladaptive ways to stress, but as they encounter various challenges, they learn from these experiences. This learning process often involves recognizing their limitations and working to overcome them. Such a journey showcases a character's resilience and determination, as they strive to modify their future responses to stress. This evolution not only adds depth to the character but also resonates with readers, who often seek stories of overcoming adversity and personal growth.

5. Interpersonal Dynamics Under Stress:

Under the pressure of stress, interpersonal dynamics within a narrative can undergo significant shifts, often serving as a catalyst for conflict or growth. Stress can strain relationships, leading to conflicts and misunderstandings, as characters react under pressure, revealing hidden tensions or unresolved issues. Equally, these high-pressure situations can also deepen bonds, as characters find mutual support and understanding in the face of adversity.

In group settings, such as teams or communities, the way characters respond to stress can greatly influence the overall dynamics. It can reveal natural leaders who step up in crisis, followers who look for guidance, mediators who strive to maintain harmony, and dissenters who challenge the status quo. These dynamics are crucial in shaping the narrative, as they can lead to pivotal moments of conflict resolution, character development, and plot progression.

> What kind of character would you make? Personally, I always step up in the leadership position when no one else wants to, but when someone else does step up, I normally avoid that specific conflict and just follow, normally not being nearly as productive as I would've been if I was in the leadership position.

6. Crafting Authentic Stress Reactions:

In crafting authentic stress reactions for characters, a blend of research and empathy is essential. Understanding real-world psychological impacts of stress and various coping mechanisms can provide a solid foundation for depicting realistic responses. This research can involve delving into psychological studies, reading personal accounts, or consulting with mental health professionals to gain a deeper understanding of how different individuals react under pressure.

However, it's equally important to ensure that these stress reactions are consistent with each character's development arc. While characters can evolve and change over the course of a story, their reactions to stress should align with their personality, background, and the experiences they've undergone within the narrative. This consistency helps maintain believability and allows readers to connect with the characters on a deeper level, understanding their actions and reactions as part of a coherent and evolving character journey.

Stress, in its many forms, acts as a mirror, reflecting characters' deepest fears, strengths, weaknesses, and potentials. As authors, weaving these reactions into our narratives not only adds layers of authenticity but also propels character arcs, making them dynamic and relatable. In the end, it's often in the furnace of crisis that characters are forged, emerging stronger, wiser, and more human. By understanding and harnessing the power of stress reactions, we can craft narratives that resonate with the timeless themes of struggle, resilience, and tr ansformation.

Chapter 4
The physical aspects

The Mirror of Society's Biases and a Character's Self-Perception

In the realm of storytelling, a character's physical appearance isn't just a superficial detail. It's a powerful tool that can shape their interactions, influence their self-perception, and reflect societal biases. Let's delve into the multifaceted implications of physicality and appearance in character development.

1. Societal Biases and Stereotypes:
   - Judging the Book by its Cover: Society often makes snap judgments based on appearance. Characters with conventionally attractive features might be treated more favorably, while those with unconventional or unique features might face prejudice or discrimination.

   - Cultural Standards of Beauty: Different cultures have varied standards of beauty and attractiveness. A character might be considered beautiful in one culture but not in another, leading to complex dynamics when they interact with diverse groups.

   - Age, Gender, and Race: Characters might face biases based on their age, gender, race, or ethnicity. For instance, an older character might be dismissed as out-of-touch, or a character of a particular race might face stereotypes associated with their ethnicity.

2. Self-Perception and Internal Conflicts:
- Mirror of the Soul: How characters perceive themselves can be a reflection of their internal struggles. A character might feel disconnected from their appearance, leading to issues of identity and self-worth.

- Body Image Issues: Characters might grapple with societal standards of beauty, leading to body image issues, low self-esteem, or even disorders like anorexia or body dysmorphia.

- Scars and Markings: Physical scars or unique markings can serve as reminders of past traumas or significant events, influencing a character's behavior and choices.

3. Interactions and Relationships:
- First Impressions: A character's appearance can shape first impressions, influencing initial interactions. For instance, a character dressed in rags might be dismissed as unimportant, while one in regal attire might command respect.

- Romantic Interactions: Physical attraction can play a role in romantic dynamics. However, it's essential to delve deeper, exploring emotional and intellectual connections beyond mere appearance.

- Power Dynamics: Appearance can influence power dynamics, especially in settings where attire or physical attributes denote rank or status. The business man with the most expensive suit might very well have the upper hand in high stakes talks.

4. Evolution Over Time:

- Physical Changes: As characters age or undergo significant events, their appearance might change, reflecting their growth and experiences. This can influence their self-perception and interactions. Remember this when you create character ARC across a long-running series.

- Adapting to Biases: Characters might adapt their appearance to navigate societal biases, such as changing their attire to fit into a particular group or altering their looks to avoid discrimination.

Physicality and appearance are not mere descriptive details; they are narrative tools that can shape a character's journey, reflect societal biases, and influence interactions. As authors, it's crucial to approach these aspects with sensitivity and depth, recognizing the profound impact they can have on a character's life and the broader narrative. By doing so, we can craft characters that resonate with authenticity, challenge societal norms, and offer readers a mirror to reflect on their biases and perceptions, without being preachy.

> *"The world is a diverse place. Fiction should be, too."*—**Mark Allan Gunnells, When It Rains**

Character Voice and Dialogue

In the world of storytelling, dialogue is like a superpower for authors. It's how characters jump off the page, showing who they are, where they've been, and what's going on in their heads. But it's not just about the words they say; it's how they say them. The way a character speaks—their choice of words, their tone, their speaking style—tells us a lot about them. Although we'll discuss dialogue in much more depth in Shadows & Ink Vol.2, let's quickly dive into the world of character voices and dialogue, and see just how important they are in bringing stories and characters to life.

The Essence of Character Voice:
When it comes to the essence of character voice, think of it as each character's signature tune. Just like everyone has their own way of talking, each character in your story should have a distinct manner of expression. This isn't just about what they say, but how they say it. Their speech patterns, choice of words, and even their tone can tell a story of their own. Imagine a character's voice as a window into their world. It can reveal bits about their upbringing, education, and cultural roots. Whether it's a unique accent, a local dialect, or specific phrases they use, these details do more than just differentiate characters; they breathe life into them, making them stand out and stay with the reader.

The Power of Tone:
The power of tone in a character's voice is like a hidden layer of communication, subtly revealing their inner emotional landscape. It's not just about the words they choose, but the way they're delivered. A character's tone can be a window into their soul, showing us what's really going on beneath the surface. For instance, a sarcastic remark might be a shield for pain, or an overly cheerful response could be a mask for anxiety. Even a seemingly calm tone might be the quiet before a storm of anger. Beyond expressing their own feelings, the tone a character uses can also reflect their relationships with others. It can convey warmth, indifference, hostility, or affection, offering a glimpse into the complexities of their interactions and connections with the world around them.

Rhythm and Pace:
Rhythm and pace in dialogue do more than just convey words; they mirror a

character's inner workings. The way a character speaks can be a direct reflection of their thoughts and emotions. For instance, a character who speaks slowly and hesitantly might be revealing their uncertainty or careful consideration. On the other hand, someone who rattles off dialogue at a breakneck pace could be showing their excitement, nervousness, or even an attempt to overwhelm others. This aspect of dialogue is also a powerful tool for building tension in a scene. Short, clipped sentences can create a sense of urgency or suspense, making readers hang on to every word.

Long, meandering sentences can draw readers into a character's introspective journey, slowing down the pace to let them fully immerse in the character's thoughts and feelings.

Choice of Words:
The words a character chooses to use—or avoid—can be a window into their personality and inner world. A character who leans toward verbose, complex language might come across as intellectual, perhaps even a bit pompous, showcasing their education or a desire to impress. In contrast, a character who sticks to simple, direct sentences might be seen as straightforward, perhaps blunt, valuing clarity over embellishment. But it's not just about the words spoken—it's also about the silences, the things left unsaid. When a character evades a question, offers half-truths, or omits key details, they're not just filling space in the dialogue. They're hinting at deeper secrets, regrets, or hidden agendas, which are so important in suspense and horror writing. These unspoken elements can be just as telling, if not more so, than the words they choose to share, adding layers of complexity and intrigue to their character.

Consistency is Key:
Consistency in a character's voice is crucial for maintaining authenticity. As characters grow and evolve, their fundamental way of speaking should stay true to their nature. Abrupt or unexplained shifts in dialogue style can disorient

readers, breaking the spell of the narrative. It's this steady, recognizable voice that anchors a character in the reader's mind, making them believable and relatable throughout their journey.

Dialogue as a Tool:
Dialogue serves as a dynamic tool in storytelling, adept at both propelling the plot forward and deepening character development. It can subtly reveal key plot points, introduce new conflicts, or hint at future events, keeping readers engaged and curious. Simultaneously, it provides a window into the characters' minds, allowing them to confront their flaws, reflect on their growth, and experience moments of realization. This dual function of dialogue enriches the narrative, making it a vital element in crafting a compelling story. Dialogue can be used to summarize an entire flashback scene, but be careful that it doesn't turn into an info dump.

Dialogue is the heartbeat of a narrative, pulsating with emotions, revelations, and dynamics. Crafting authentic character voices is akin to composing a symphony, where each instrument has its unique sound, yet together they create a harmonious ensemble. As authors, our challenge is to ensure that each character's voice rings true, resonating with authenticity and depth.

Chapter 5
Backstory Development

A character's backstory is like a hidden layer underneath everything they do, think, and feel in your story. It's all their past experiences, relationships, wins, and losses that make them who they are when your readers first bump into them. Getting into a character's backstory does more than just fill in blanks; it gives their actions and choices a reason and makes them more real and easier to connect with. Let's dive into how to put together a great backstory for your characters.

Past Traumas:

- Defining Moments: Traumatic events can serve as defining moments in a character's life, influencing their fears, motivations, and behaviors. Whether it's a personal loss, an accident, or a betrayal, these events can leave lasting scars.

- Coping Mechanisms: How a character copes with trauma can reveal a lot about their personality. Some might turn to vices, some might become withdrawn, while others might channel their pain into determination and drive (I am *so* the latter).

Achievements:

- Milestones: Celebratory moments, like academic achievements, professional successes, or personal milestones, can shape a character's self-worth and confidence.

- Skills and Talents: A character's achievements can also highlight their skills, talents, and passions, providing insights into their strengths and capabilities.

Relationships:
- Family Ties: Family dynamics, including sibling rivalries, parental expectations, or ancestral legacies, can influence a character's values, beliefs, and aspirations.

- Romantic Histories: Past romances, heartbreaks, and partnerships can shape a character's approach to love, trust, and commitment.

- Friendships: Lifelong friendships, betrayals, or mentorships can offer insights into a character's loyalty, trustworthiness, and interpersonal skills.

Turning Points:
- Decisions and Regrets: Key decisions, whether they led to success or regret, can serve as turning points, influencing a character's future choices and their perception of right and wrong.

- Life-Changing Events: Events like relocating to a new place, changing careers, or experiencing a significant loss can drastically alter a character's trajectory, priorities, and worldview.

Personal Beliefs and Values:
- Cultural and Religious Influences: A character's cultural background and religious beliefs can shape their morals, traditions, and perspectives.

- Philosophical Stances: Personal philosophies, political beliefs, or ethical stances can influence a character's decisions, allegiances, and conflicts.

A character's backstory is like the roots of a tree, hidden beneath the surface but providing the essential nourishment and stability for the visible growth above. As authors, crafting a detailed and nuanced backstory is akin to laying the foundation for a house. It might not always be explicitly visible in the narrative, but its presence is felt in every corner, every room, and every brick. By investing time in developing a rich backstory, authors ensure that their characters resonate with authenticity, depth, and humanity, making them unforgettable in the minds of readers.

"Be regular and orderly in your life, so that you may be violent and original in your work."—**Clive Barker**

Character Relationships

Storytelling is a lot like a dance, and the relationships between characters are the steps that make it interesting. These connections—be they filled with conflict, support, love, or rivalry—are what give the story its texture and depth. They're not just there for drama. They shape the plot and drive the characters to make decisions, change, and grow. Let's jump into the rich and complex world of character relationships and see how they really make a story come to life.

Friendships:
- Friendships that endure through the years are more than just connections—they're a testament to loyalty, shared memories, and mutual

evolution. These lifelong bonds often act as a steadfast anchor for characters, offering unwavering support and understanding during their most challenging moments, and highlighting the enduring power of deep, lasting relationships in shaping a character's journey.

- Some friendships, unlike those built on deep connections, are formed on the basis of convenience or superficial ties. These fair-weather friendships often lack the resilience to withstand life's pressures and challenges. When tested, they may unravel, leading to conflicts and eye-opening revelations, and revealing the true nature of the relationship and the characters involved.

Rivalries:
- Rivalries, whether rooted in professional ambitions, personal vendettas, or romantic entanglements, often act as a catalyst in a character's journey. These competitive dynamics push characters to their limits, revealing not just their determination and resilience, but also exposing their vulnerabilities and weaknesses. Such rivalries can be a powerful tool in storytelling, highlighting the multifaceted nature of characters and the complexities of their motivations and actions.

- Over time, the fiery intensity of rivalries can transform, leading to unexpected alliances or even blossoming friendships. This evolution in relationships underscores the fluidity and complexity of human connections. It highlights the potential for growth, understanding, and change, even among the most unlikely of characters. Such dynamics enrich the narrative, offering a nuanced exploration of how adversarial relationships can evolve into something more profound and meaningful.

Romances:

- In the early chapters of a romance subplot, where hearts flutter and sparks fly, we get a glimpse into the deeper layers of a character's soul. This phase, brimming with attraction and infatuation, lays bare their vulnerabilities, unspoken desires, and hopeful dreams. It's a time when characters are most open, revealing not just who they are but who they wish to be, as they navigate the exhilarating, often tumultuous waters of newfound love. A romance subplot works great for a horror novel, since it just adds that extra layer of empathy for the character. We've all been in love before.

- As romance evolves from its initial rush into deeper waters, it inevitably encounters the swirling currents of challenges—misunderstandings, external pressures, and personal demons. This phase is a true test of the characters' bond. How they navigate these hurdles, whether they falter or find strength in each other, speaks volumes about their commitment and the depth of their feelings. It's in these moments of struggle and resolution that the true resilience and substance of their relationship are revealed.

- In the realm of horror, where darkness often mirrors reality, failed romances can be a crucible for transformation. The end of a love affair, especially in a genre that delves into the macabre and the unsettling, can lead characters down a path of introspection and self-discovery. It's in the ashes of these failed relationships that characters often find the grit to emerge stronger, more resilient, and sometimes, with a newfound understanding of themselves and the twisted world they inhabit. This journey through heartbreak and its aftermath can add a profound layer of depth to horror narratives, resonating with the stark realities of life and loss.

Family Ties:

- Parents in a character's backstory are huge. They shape who your character is, from their deepest beliefs to what they dream of becoming. These relationships can be a bit messy, full of misunderstandings and unmet expectations. In horror, this can really amp up the tension. Your character might be desperate for their parent's approval or trying to break away from family expectations. How they deal with these family issues can add a lot of depth to their story, especially in horror where family can be a source of strength or a spooky burden.

- Sibling relationships are a rollercoaster of emotions. They've got elements of rivalry and friendship, mixed with a shared past that's hard to shake off. In horror, these relationships can really hit hard. Siblings might band together against a frightening foe or find themselves at odds with each other. Exploring these bonds can reveal a lot about your character, like how they handle family pressures or deep-rooted secrets. Sibling interactions are great for adding emotional layers and conflict to your story, making these relationships a key part of building your characters.

- When it comes to adding layers to your character's world, don't forget about extended family like aunts, uncles, and grandparents. They can bring a mix of support, wisdom, and sometimes, a whole lot of drama. In horror stories, these characters can be crucial. They might hold on to ancient family secrets, offer sage advice, or stir up problems. How they interact with your main characters can reveal hidden family histories and introduce complex storylines. This extended family network expands the world your character lives in, giving a richer, more detailed backdrop for their journey. Whether they're helping out against eerie forces or adding to the family drama, they play a big part in the web of relationships that drive your story forward.

Mentorships and Proteges:

- In the realm of horror fiction, mentor-protege relationships often play a crucial role, highlighting the transfer of knowledge, skills, and values in a high-stakes environment. These dynamics can be particularly compelling, as they often involve the passing down of arcane knowledge, survival skills, or secret techniques necessary to confront supernatural threats. The mentor, typically a figure with a wealth of experience and wisdom, guides the protege, who is usually less experienced but eager to learn. This relationship is not just about skill transfer. It's also about the emotional and psychological growth of both characters.

- Challenges often arise as the protege grows more capable and independent, leading to tensions over independence and the mentor's struggle to let go. In horror narratives, these tensions can be heightened by the life-or-death stakes involved. The protege's journey to forge their path can involve not only mastering the skills taught but also confronting and overcoming fears and moral dilemmas that the mentor may have faced in the past. This dynamic adds a layer of depth to the story, as it explores themes of legacy, the burden of knowledge, and the cyclical nature of mentorship within the chilling context of horror.

- Mentorships can sometimes veer into darker territories, where betrayals or clashing ideologies lead to intense rifts and conflicts. These betrayals can be particularly jarring and impactful, as they often come from a trusted figure who has provided guidance and support. The reasons for betrayal can vary widely, from a mentor's hidden agenda or corruption to ideological differences that become insurmountable. Such betrayals can be a pivotal moment in a story, forcing the protege to question their beliefs, reassess their values, and often, confront their mentor. This dynamic adds a layer of complexity to the narrative, as it delves into themes of trust, disillusionment, and the painful realization that those who teach us the most can also hurt us deeply (think of the *Batman Begins* movie). In the context of horror, these betrayals can have life-altering or even life-threatening consequences, heightening the tension and emotional stakes of the story.

Think of relationships in your stories as mirrors. They reflect the best and worst parts of your characters, challenging them, supporting them, and sometimes breaking them down only to build them up again in new ways. As a writer, especially in horror, it's crucial to weave these authentic, evolving relationships into your narrative. They add a layer of realism and emotional depth that's hard to beat. Your characters are defined not just by who they are on their own, but also by how they interact, respond, and grow with others (like my parents always said, "We can be judged purely by who our friends are."). In the end, it's these complex dynamics that make your stories hit home, echoing the real-life ties, conflicts, and connections we all experience.

The Role of Social Class, Worldview, Upbringing, and Education

When you're spinning the yarn of your story, remember that characters are more than just pawns moving your plot along. They're like real people, with all the messy, intricate bits that make us human. To create characters that truly connect with your readers, especially in horror where the human element is so vital, you've got to dig deep. Get to know them inside out. What's their social standing? How do they see the world? What was their childhood like? How educated are they? These aren't just details—they're the building blocks of a believable character. Since we've already talked about most of these, I'll keep it short as we dive into why these aspects are so important in breathing life into your characters.

1. Social Class:
   - Economic Implications: A character's social class can determine their access to resources, their occupation, and their overall lifestyle. A character from an affluent background will navigate the world differently from one who has faced economic hardships.

   - Interpersonal Dynamics: Social class can influence a character's interactions with others, shaping their friendships, romances, and conflicts. It can lead to tensions, alliances, or even romances that cross class boundaries.

   - Internal Conflicts: Characters might grapple with their social standing, aspiring for more or feeling guilt over their privilege.

2. Worldview:
   - Moral Compass: A character's worldview defines their beliefs about right and wrong, influencing their decisions and actions throughout the story.

   - Interactions with Others: Characters with differing worldviews can lead to rich dialogues, debates, and conflicts, adding depth to the narrative.

   - Evolution of Beliefs: As characters encounter new experiences, their worldviews might be challenged, leading to personal growth and transformation.

3. Upbringing:
  - Formative Experiences: Early life experiences, family dynamics, and childhood memories can shape a character's fears, desires, and motivations.

  - Cultural and Traditional Influences: A character's upbringing will determine their cultural practices, rituals, and values, adding layers to their identity.

  - Traumas and Triumphs: Past traumas or successes can influence a character's present actions, serving as obstacles or driving forces in their journey.

4. Education:
  - Knowledge and Skills: A character's education can equip them with specific skills, knowledge, and expertise, influencing their profession, hobbies, and problem-solving approaches. Think of all the stories where street orphans learned to pickpocket and be resourceful.

  - Social Interactions: Educational institutions serve as social melting pots. Characters might form lifelong friendships, rivalries, or romances during their educational years.

  - Personal Growth: Education can be a period of self-discovery, where characters grapple with their identities, beliefs, and aspirations.

Characters, like real individuals, are products of their environments, experiences, and choices. By weaving elements of social class, worldview, upbringing, and education into their backstories, authors can craft multi-dimensional characters that mirror the complexities of real life. These elements not only add depth to the characters but also make them relatable, allowing readers to see reflections of their struggles, aspirations, and dilemmas. In essence, understanding these facets is not just about character development. It's about capturing the essence of the human experience.

Navigating Cultural Differences in Characters

In today's globalized world, literature often serves as a bridge between cultures, offering readers a window into lives, experiences, and perspectives different from their own. However, when authors venture into depicting characters from cultures or backgrounds different from theirs, it's crucial to approach the task with sensitivity, respect, and diligence. Here's a guide to help authors navigate cultural differences in their characters responsibly:

1. Do Thorough Research:
When you're aiming to represent a culture accurately in your writing, especially in horror where authenticity adds to the eeriness, doing your homework is key. Start by diving into primary sources—think books, documentaries, and articles created by people from within the culture itself. This approach gives you a genuine, insider's perspective. But don't stop there. It's also a smart move to chat with cultural experts or sensitivity readers. They can guide you, helping ensure that your portrayal is not just accurate, but also respectful and nuanced. This kind of thorough research is the backbone of authentic cultural representation in your storytelling.

2. Avoid Stereotypes and Clichés:
When crafting characters, especially in the horror genre where every detail counts, it's crucial to steer clear of stereotypes and clichés. Stereotypes are like shortcuts—oversimplified and generalized beliefs about a group that can perpetuate harmful biases and misconceptions. They lack the depth and nuance

that make characters truly come alive and resonate with readers. To break free from these constraints, focus on portraying each character as a unique individual, not just a representative of their culture. This approach not only enriches your story but also respects the diversity and complexity of real people. Remember, in horror, authenticity in characters can make the difference between a forgettable tale and one that lingers in the mind long after the last page is turned. We'll dive even deeper into stereotypes later on.

3. Respect Cultural Significance:

When integrating cultural elements into your horror narrative, it's vital to approach them with respect and understanding. Before weaving practices, rituals, or symbols into your story, take the time to comprehend their cultural, historical, and spiritual significance. This depth of understanding ensures that these elements are not reduced to mere plot devices or exotic backdrops. Instead, they should serve a meaningful and integral role in your story, enhancing the narrative's authenticity and depth.

4. Showcase Diversity Within the Culture:

In the realm of writing (any realm, actually), showcasing the diversity within a culture is crucial. Every cultural or ethnic group is a mosaic of varied beliefs, practices, and experiences. Recognizing and depicting this range adds layers of authenticity and depth to your narrative. It's important to steer clear of portraying any culture as monolithic or homogenous. By doing so, you not only enrich your story but also pay homage to the complexities and nuances of real-world cultures. This approach ensures that your horror tales resonate with a sense of realism and respect, offering readers a more immersive and thoughtful experience.

5. Be Mindful of Language:

When crafting characters, being mindful of language is paramount. If your characters speak a language different from the primary language of your narrative, it's essential to ensure accurate translations. Avoid trivializing or mocking accents or dialects, as this can detract from the authenticity and respectfulness of your portrayal. Additionally, pay close attention to the implications and nuances of specific terms or phrases. Some words might carry cultural sensitivity or historical connotations that could unintentionally offend or misrepresent. Thoughtful and respectful use of language not only enhances the credibility of your characters but also enriches the overall narrative, making it more engaging and respectful to diverse readerships. You want your book to be an international success, right?

6. Understand the Power Dynamics:
Understanding the power dynamics between cultures is crucial, especially when delving into themes like colonization, oppression, or discrimination. As an author, it's important to be acutely aware of both historical and present-day power imbalances. When you're touching on these sensitive themes, approach them with deep empathy and awareness. Ensure that your narrative doesn't inadvertently perpetuate harmful biases or stereotypes. This careful consideration not only adds depth and authenticity to your story but also respects the complexities of real-world issues. It's about striking a balance between crafting a compelling, spine-chilling tale and being mindful of the broader implications of the cultural contexts you explore.

7. Reflect on Your Motivations:
When you decide to write about a culture different from your own, it's vital to reflect deeply on your motivations. Ask yourself: Why am I drawn to this particular culture? Ensure that your interest stems from a place of genuine respect and a desire to understand and uplift, rather than to appropriate or exoticize. This introspection is key to creating a narrative that's not only respectful and authentic but also enriches your story with depth and sincerity.

It's about weaving a tale that honors the culture you're portraying, while still sending shivers down the spine of your readers.

8. Be Open to Feedback:
Once you've written your story, it's vital to get feedback from people who are part of the culture you're writing about. Their views can make a big difference in ensuring that you're showing their culture accurately and respectfully. Be ready to listen closely to what they say, and don't shy away from tweaking your story based on their suggestions. Understand that no story can capture everything about a culture. So it's important to be humble and realize that your view has its limits. Being open to learning not only makes your story better but also shows respect for the culture you're including in your narrative.

When you include different cultures in your writing, it's more than just storytelling. It's a way to help people understand and connect with each other. But with that comes the responsibility to get it right—to be respectful and detailed. By putting in the effort, being humble, and really wanting to learn, writers can create characters that not only feel real to readers but also celebrate the diverse cultures they come from.

> Success in writing isn't measured by sales alone, but by the stories you tell and the hearts you touch.

Chapter 6

Arcs

Planning a Character's Arc

A character's arc is the journey of transformation or growth they undergo throughout a story or series. It's the backbone that gives depth to the narrative, making characters relatable and their journeys compelling. Crafting a well-defined arc is essential for creating characters that resonate with readers.

Here's a guide to planning a character's arc:

- Understand the Types of Character Arcs

- Identify the Starting Point

- Determine the End Point

- Chart the Key Milestones

- Integrate Subplots and Relationships

- Ensure Organic Growth

- Re-evaluate and Adjust

- Consider Long-Term Arcs for Series

- Reflect Real Emotions and Struggles

- Revise and Refine

Now let's dive into each one:

Understand the Types of Character Arcs:
- Positive Growth Arc: Here, we see characters grow into a better version of themselves. They face and overcome things like personal fears, mistakes, or wrong beliefs, and sometimes they tackle outside challenges, too. This journey of growing and getting stronger is usually a key part of the story and can be uplifting and rewarding for us as readers. We often end up rooting for these characters because they adapt and show real guts, making them feel real and likable.

- Negative or Tragic Arc: This is the flip side of the positive growth arc. In these stories, characters might have some serious flaws or make bad decisions, or maybe they're just dealt a tough hand by life. Whatever the reason, they end up facing a downfall or a really sad ending. These stories dive into the darker sides of what it means to be human and the consequences of our choices. They can be pretty heavy, but they're also really moving and can make us think deeply about life and our choices.

- Flat Arc: In a flat arc, the character doesn't really change much themselves. Instead, their strong beliefs or personality traits have a big impact on the world or people around them. These stories are interesting because they focus on a character who sticks to their guns, no matter what's happening around them. It shows how someone who's true to themselves can make a difference in their world, even if they don't go through a huge personal change.

Identify the Starting Point:

- Establish the Status Quo: Where is the character at the beginning of the story? What are their beliefs, fears, desires, and flaws?

- Inciting Incident: Identify the pivotal event that disrupts the character's normal life, propelling them onto an uncharted trajectory. For instance, in a fantasy tale, this could be the discovery of a hidden power or a call to embark on a perilous quest. This moment is crucial as it not only challenges their current state but also serves as the driving force behind their transformative journey throughout the narrative.

Determine the End Point:

- Envision where your character should stand at the story's or series' conclusion. Consider whether they have realized their aspirations, undergone a transformation in their perspectives, or fulfilled their destined path. This end point is crucial in shaping their journey and the narrative's overall impact.

Chart the Key Milestones:

- First Act Turn: The character makes a choice that sets them on the path of their arc.

- Midpoint: A significant event that either challenges the character's beliefs or pushes them further toward their transformation.

- Dark Night of the Soul: The character's lowest point, where all seems lost or they confront their deepest fears.

- Climax: The character's beliefs and growth are tested in a final confrontation or challenge.

- Resolution: The character's arc reaches its conclusion, showcasing their growth or regression.

Integrate Subplots and Relationships:

- Integrating subplots and relationships into the main narrative is a crucial aspect of crafting a compelling and richly layered story. Subplots, when woven skillfully into the main plot, can significantly enhance the depth and complexity of the narrative. They provide additional dimensions to the protagonist's journey, offering insights into their character and the world they inhabit.

- Secondary characters, such as allies, mentors, antagonists, and love interests, are not just mere additions to the story. They are integral in shaping the protagonist's arc. These characters bring their own backgrounds, motivations, and conflicts, which can intersect with the main plot in meaningful ways. For instance, a mentor's wisdom or an antagonist's opposition can be pivotal in pushing the protagonist toward growth or presenting them with formidable challenges.

- Moreover, subplots can serve as a mirror to the main plot, highlighting themes or presenting contrasting perspectives. They add layers of intrigue and keep the readers engaged, as they unfold alongside the main story. A well-crafted subplot can also provide necessary relief from the main narrative's tension, offering a change of pace and keeping the story dynamic.

The art of intertwining subplots and relationships with the main plot lies in their ability to enrich the narrative without overshadowing it. They should feel like natural extensions of the story, contributing to the protagonist's journey and the overall thematic resonance of the book. A great book often owes its success to these intricately woven subplots that create a tapestry of interconnected stories, each adding to the richness of the narrative universe.

Ensure Organic Growth:
- For a character's development to feel genuine, avoid abrupt or unexplained changes in their behavior. Each progression in their arc should naturally stem from their experiences, decisions, and the repercussions of these actions.

Re-evaluate and Adjust:
- As your story unfolds, periodically reassess your character's development. Make sure their actions consistently reflect their growth, ensuring that their transformation is believable and well-deserved.

Consider Long-Term Arcs for Series:
- When embarking on the journey of writing a series, it's essential to meticulously plan not just the arc of each individual book but also the overarching narrative that spans the entire series. This dual-layered approach ensures that each installment contributes meaningfully to the character's journey, while also maintaining a sense of continuity and progression across the series. By carefully crafting these long-term arcs, authors can keep readers deeply engaged, eagerly anticipating how each book advances the larger story, and how the characters evolve throughout the series. This strategic planning is key to creating a compelling and cohesive series that captivates its audience from the first book to the last. It'll also prevent the need of multiple rereads and rewrites for yourself.

Reflect Real Emotions and Struggles:

- To create a truly compelling character arc, it's vital to root it in authentic emotions, realistic challenges, and meaningful growth. This approach ensures that the character's transformation resonates deeply with readers, making it not just a narrative device, but a relatable and impactful journey. By focusing on genuine emotional experiences and realistic obstacles, the character's evolution becomes a mirror for the human experience, allowing readers to connect with and be moved by the character's journey. This emotional grounding is what transforms a good character arc into a memorable and powerful story element.

Revise and Refine:

- When crafting a character's journey, especially in a series, it's crucial to maintain consistency and depth throughout. After completing the story or series, revisit the character's arc during the revision process. This is the time to ensure that the character's growth or decline is clearly depicted and remains consistent across the narrative. An effective way to track this is by creating a character arc timeline or chart, where you can visually map out key moments of change, challenges faced, and how these experiences have shaped the character. This visual aid helps in identifying any inconsistencies or gaps in the character's development, ensuring a coherent and compelling arc from start to finish.

In conclusion, a character's arc is a vital element in storytelling, providing depth, emotion, and a sense of journey. By meticulously planning and integrating this arc into the narrative, authors can craft characters that live, breathe, and evolve, leaving a lasting impression on readers.

Chapter 7

Taking your characters to the next level

Testing Actions Against Character Traits

Ensuring that a character's actions align with their established traits is crucial for maintaining authenticity in storytelling. While we've touched on some methods, let's delve deeper into various ways an author can test actions against character traits:

Role-Playing Scenarios:
Put yourself in the character's shoes and role-play the scenario. Would they react the way you've written, given their background, beliefs, and experiences? I once had the privilege of acting students doing a reading of one of my stories years back. They had a few days to prepare, so there was real emotion in their words, and we quickly spotted any remaining issues with the story, dialogue, and even the narrative. *Highly* recommended.

Character Interviews (again):
Conduct an "interview" with your character. Ask them why they took a particular action and listen to their "response." This can help clarify motivations and

ensure alignment with their traits. See it as a police interview after the events of the book.

Peer Review and Feedback:
Share specific scenes with fellow writers or beta readers and ask if the character's actions feel authentic. Sometimes, an external perspective can catch inconsistencies the author might overlook.

Compare with Past Behavior:
Review past scenes or situations where the character faced similar dilemmas or emotions. Are their reactions consistent? If not, is there a justified reason for the change?

Emotional and Psychological Consistency:
Consider the character's current emotional and psychological state. Even if an action seems slightly out of character, it might be justified by their mental state at that moment.

Challenge with Contradictory Situations:
Place the character in a situation that directly challenges one of their core traits. Their reaction can reveal deeper layers of their personality and test the strength of their established traits.

Utilize Character Surveys or Quizzes:
Use real-world personality tests (like the Myers-Briggs Type Indicator) tailored to your character. Their results can offer insights into how they might react in certain situations.

Mind Mapping:
Create a mind map that branches out from a particular action or decision. Each

branch represents a possible reaction based on different character traits. This can help visualize the most authentic path for the character.

Revisit Character Backstory:
Reflect on the character's backstory. Past traumas, joys, relationships, and experiences can heavily influence present actions.

The "Three Whys" Technique:
For any significant action, ask "Why?" three times to drill down into the deeper motivations. For example, "Why did she run away?" "Because she was scared." "Why was she scared?" "Because she recognized one of the attackers." "Why did she recognize them?" "They were from her past."

Contrast with Other Characters:
Compare the action in question with how other characters in the story might react. This can highlight whether the action is unique and authentic to the character or a generic response.

Reflect on Theme and Symbolism:
Sometimes, a character's action might serve a symbolic purpose or reflect the broader theme of the story. Ensure that such actions, while serving the narrative, don't betray the character's essence.

In essence, testing actions against character traits is a multi-faceted process that requires deep introspection, creativity, and a thorough understanding of the character's psyche. By employing a combination of these techniques, authors can craft authentic, consistent, and compelling character-driven narratives.

Stereotypes

Characters should be multi-dimensional. Even if they have dominant traits, they can still have moments of doubt, vulnerability, or contradiction.

Stereotypes, broadly defined, are oversimplified and generalized beliefs or ideas about a particular group of people or things. They arise from a human tendency to categorize and simplify complex information to make sense of the world. While they can sometimes be based on a grain of truth, stereotypes often distort or exaggerate reality, leading to misconceptions and biases.

Origins of Stereotypes: Stereotypes have deep historical and sociological roots. They emerge from:

- Cultural Narratives: Think about the old tales and legends that have been around for ages. These stories are more than just bedtime tales—they actually shape how we see certain groups of people. They're like family heirlooms, passing down beliefs about different communities, sometimes in ways that aren't exactly fair or true.

- Media Representation: How groups of people are shown in movies, TV shows, and books really matters. Back in the day, media often showed certain ethnicities or genders in a bad light, and that's stuck around. These old-school portrayals didn't give the full picture, and they ended up creating some pretty stubborn stereotypes.

- Human Cognitive Processes: Our brains like to keep things simple, so they lump information into categories. This is handy but can lead us to make big generalizations, especially if we don't have a lot of real-life experience with different kinds of people. It's like our brains take shortcuts, but sometimes these shortcuts miss the mark.

- Evolution of Stereotypes: Stereotypes change as time goes by. As our world gets more connected and cultures mix, the old stereotypes can get a refresh or fade away. This change is influenced by a few things:

- Increased Exposure: When we meet and hang out with people from different walks of life, we start to see that our old beliefs might not be spot-on. Getting to know people personally helps bust myths and stereotypes.

- Sociopolitical Movements: Big movements like feminism and civil rights have really shaken up some old stereotypes. They push for fairness and show that a lot of stereotypes just don't hold water.

- Modern Media: Nowadays, media is everywhere, and it's got a lot of power in shaping how we think. With so many people tuning in from all over the world, media can keep stereotypes going or help knock them down. The good news is, we're starting to see more diverse stories and characters, which is helping change some outdated views.

Stereotypes in Horror Fiction: Horror, as a genre, often plays on societal fears, and in doing so, it sometimes leans into stereotypes. Common stereotypes in horror include:

- The Expendable Sidekick: Often a person of color, this character usually dies first.

- The Damsel in Distress: A female character who exists solely to be saved.

- The Mad Scientist: An embodiment of the fear of unchecked ambition or science gone awry.

- The "Foreign" Threat: Villains or monsters from exotic, often Eastern, locales, playing on xenophobic fears.

- The Cursed Artifact: An object, often from a non-Western culture, that brings doom to its possessor.

Using or Avoiding Stereotypes in Horror:
- Writers should be aware of common stereotypes and critically assess whether they're perpetuating harmful narratives.

- Use the stereotype as a starting point, then subvert it. For instance, the "damsel" could turn out to be the most resourceful character.

- If a character seems to fit a stereotype on the surface, give them depth and layers that challenge the stereotype as the story unfolds.

- If drawing from different cultures, do thorough research. Avoid reducing rich cultures to mere horror props.

- Diverse beta readers can provide insights into potential stereotypical portrayals.

While stereotypes have been a part of storytelling for ages, modern writers bear the responsibility of thoughtful and sensitive portrayal. Horror, with its exploration of societal fears, has a unique opportunity to challenge and reshape these narratives. By doing so, it can not only provide scares but also promote understanding and empathy.

"You don't write because you want to say something, you write because you have something to say."—**F. Scott Fitzgerald**

The Importance of Tracking World and Setting Rules in Fiction

In the realm of fiction, especially genres that delve into fantastical worlds or intricate settings, the environment in which the story unfolds becomes as essential as the characters themselves. Whether it's the sprawling landscapes of Middle-Earth, the magical laws governing Hogwarts, or the dystopian society of Panem, the setting and its rules can shape the narrative, influence character actions, and captivate readers. But how does an author ensure consistency and depth in such complex worlds? The answer lies in meticulous tracking and documentation.

World-building is an art. It's the process of constructing an imaginary world, complete with its geography, history, cultures, and rules. This world, once created, becomes the stage upon which characters act and the story unfolds. But unlike our consistent reality, fictional worlds exist only in the author's imagination and, subsequently, on the page. So maintaining consistency becomes crucial.

Why Track Setting and World Rules?

- Consistency: Readers invest in the reality of the story. Inconsistencies, be it in the magic system, the political hierarchy, or the way technology functions, can break immersion.

- Character Actions: The rules of the world influence how characters interact with their environment and each other. Keeping track ensures characters act in line with the world's logic.

- Plot Development: Many plots revolve around the exploration, exploitation, or subversion of world rules. Knowing these rules inside out can lead to richer plot developments.

- Depth and Immersion: A well-documented world feels lived-in and real, enhancing reader immersion.

How to Track World and Setting Rules:

- World Bible: Create a comprehensive document detailing every aspect of the world. This can include maps, character relationships, timelines, societal norms, and more.

- Rule Sheets: For worlds with magic, advanced technology, or unique phenomena like the supernatural, maintain a sheet detailing how these systems function, their limitations, and their origins.

- Cultural Dossiers: If the world has diverse cultures or species, create profiles for each, noting their customs, beliefs, attire, and any other distinguishing features.

- Setting Descriptions: Maintain detailed descriptions of key locations. This can help in ensuring that the environment remains consistent throughout the story.

- Feedback and Beta Readers: Engage readers familiar with the genre to spot inconsistencies or provide insights into world-building.

- The Balance of Flexibility and Rigidity: While tracking is essential, authors should also allow some flexibility. As the narrative evolves, some world rules might need to change to serve the story better. The key is to ensure that any change is logical, consistent, and serves the narrative's greater good. Keep a checklist for revisions, especially if you're writing a continuing series. We'll cover more on this in a bit.

The worlds authors craft are the foundations of their narratives. They're the realms where heroes rise, villains fall, and epic tales unfold. By meticulously tracking the rules and nuances of these worlds, authors not only ensure consistency but also craft a setting that lives and breathes, pulling readers into its depths and making them never want to leave.

Revise with Authenticity in Mind

When you're revising your story, it's really important to keep your characters true to themselves. Think about how they act and react. Do these actions fit with what you've already told your readers about them? Your characters should feel real. Their choices should make sense for who they are, based on their personality and what they've been through.

Take a close look at the big moments and conversations in your story. Ask yourself, "Is this what my character would really do or say?" If something feels off, like a character is doing something just to move the plot along, it might be time to change things up. Maybe tweak what happened before this moment, adjust the character's background a bit, or even rethink the whole scene. The goal is to make every action feel natural and right for that character.

Don't be afraid to make big changes if they're needed. Keeping your characters consistent makes your story more believable and engaging. It's okay if this takes a bit of extra time and effort. It's all about making your story the best it can be, with characters that your readers will believe in and care about.

Continual Reflection

Firstly, try keeping a journal as if you're your character. It's about getting into their head, understanding what they think and feel, so they stay true to themselves in your story. And make sure to check in with your characters often, especially in longer stories or series. See it as catching up with old friends to keep their stories straight and consistent.

In the vast expanse of storytelling, characters stand as the pillars that uphold the narrative. They are the heartbeat, the soul, and the voice that echo long after the last page is turned. For authors, these characters are not just figments of imagination but living entities that evolve, react, and interact within the confines of the story's world. This relationship between the author and their characters becomes even more crucial when navigating the intricate pathways of longer works or series.

The Importance of Staying Connected:

- Consistency: Characters, like real people, have core traits, beliefs, and histories. Regularly reconnecting ensures that these remain consistent, providing authenticity to the character's actions and decisions throughout the narrative.

- Evolution: While consistency is key, characters also evolve. By staying in touch, authors can chart this growth organically, ensuring it aligns with the story's events and the character's experiences.

- Emotional Depth: A deep connection allows authors to delve into the emotional depths of their characters, enriching the narrative with genuine feelings and reactions.

- Avoiding Plot Holes: Characters drive the plot. By understanding them thoroughly, authors can avoid narrative inconsistencies or actions that don't align with the character's established persona.

Ways to Stay Connected:

- Character Journals: Maintain a journal from the character's perspective. Regular entries can provide insights into their mindset, feelings, and reactions to events, ensuring the author remains attuned to their voice.

- Character Interviews: As I mentioned quite a few times, you need to periodically "interview" characters, asking them about recent events in the story, their feelings, hopes, and fears. This exercise can offer clarity on how they might react to future events. At times it might feel like a waste of time, but it will save you time in the long run, when all the edits and rewrites come into play.

- Visualization and Meditation: Dedicate quiet moments to visualize scenes from the character's viewpoint. This immersive technique can deepen the connection and understanding.

- Revisiting Past Works: If writing a series, periodically revisit earlier books or chapters. This helps in recalling the character's journey and ensures continuity.

- Feedback Loop: Engage with beta readers or writing groups, focusing specifically on character consistency and depth. External perspectives can highlight areas where the character connection might be waning.

- The Continuous Dialogue: Staying connected with characters is akin to maintaining a relationship. It requires effort, understanding, and continuous dialogue. As characters navigate the challenges, triumphs, and tribulations of the narrative, the author's unwavering connection becomes their guiding star, ensuring they remain true to themselves and the story they inhabit. In the end, it's this deep-rooted bond that translates onto the page, crafting characters that resonate, relate, and remain etched in the reader's heart.

Avoid Deus Ex Machina

Characters should solve problems or face consequences based on their abilities, knowledge, and growth, not sudden, unexplained external solutions.

The term "Deus Ex Machina" has its roots in ancient Greek theatre. Translated directly, it means "god from the machine." In classical drama, it was a common convention where a seemingly unsolvable problem in the plot was suddenly and abruptly resolved by the unexpected intervention of a god, often lowered onto the stage by a crane (the "machine"). This god would then swiftly solve the characters' dilemmas, ensuring a happy ending.

In modern storytelling, the term has evolved to refer to any sudden, unexpected solution to a seemingly insurmountable problem within a story. It's a plot device where a conflict is resolved through a means that feels contrived or out of the blue, rather than through the story's internal logic or the actions of its characters.

Imagine a story where the protagonist is trapped on an island, struggling to survive and find a way home. After numerous chapters detailing their hardships, just when things seem most dire, a previously unmentioned friendly dragon suddenly appears, offering the protagonist a ride back to their homeland. This dragon, introduced abruptly to resolve the central conflict, serves as a Deus Ex Machina.

Why Avoid Deus Ex Machina?

- Undermines Character Development: One of the joys of storytelling is watching characters grow, adapt, and overcome challenges. Relying on a Deus Ex Machina robs characters of the chance to solve problems on their own, diminishing their development and agency.

- Breaks Suspension of Disbelief: Stories, even fantastical ones, operate within a set of established rules. Introducing a sudden, unexpected solution can jolt readers out of the narrative, making them acutely aware of the story's artificiality.

- Feels Unsatisfying: Readers invest emotionally in the challenges characters face. A Deus Ex Machina can make the resolution feel unearned, leading to an unsatisfying or hollow conclusion.

- Indicates Weak Plotting: Over-reliance on this device can be seen as a sign of weak plotting or an inability to resolve conflicts in a manner consistent with the story's established world.

While Deus Ex Machina has historical roots and can occasionally be used effectively for specific thematic purposes, it's generally viewed unfavorably in modern storytelling. Authors are encouraged to find organic, character-driven solutions to conflicts, ensuring a richer and more rewarding narrative experience for readers.

Trust Your Instincts

You know your characters best. If something feels off about what they're doing, trust that feeling. It's okay to go with your gut.

The writing journey is littered with advice and rules, like this very book. Which can of course be great, especially when you're starting out. But, there's a point where following your instincts is just as important.

- Developing Your Instincts: Writing instincts don't just happen. They grow from all the time you spend writing, reading, and revising. It's like training your gut to know what's good and what's not.

- Rules Have Their Limits: Sure, rules are helpful, but they can also box you in. Writing's an art, and sometimes you gotta break the rules to make something amazing. Think about writers like James Joyce, Virginia Woolf, and Cormac McCarthy—they didn't stick to all the rules, and they wrote some pretty cool stuff.

- Too Many Rules Can Overwhelm: If you focus too much on rules, it can get overwhelming. You might start doubting yourself, overthinking, and maybe even give up on a story because you're worried about getting it "right."

- The Magic of Instinctive Writing: When you let loose and write from the heart, that's when the magic happens. That's when you write stuff that feels real and hits hard.

- Find the Right Mix: It's not about ditching all the rules. They're like a map. But don't be afraid to take a detour if your heart's telling you to. Experience comes from years of writing and, yes, doing workshops and reading On Writing books, and eventually you'll forget most of what you've learned, but it'll all be part of you by then. That's where instinct and even your voice comes from. Even then, reading an On Writing book every now and then is a great way to remind you of how far you've come. It's the same with giving back and teaching others in need.

Writing's both a skill and an art. The skill part comes from learning and following rules, but the art? That's all about your instincts and unique style. Trust yourself. The best stories often come from moments when writers listen to their guts.

Ensuring that characters act and react authentically is crucial for creating a compelling, believable narrative. By deeply understanding and staying true to each character's essence, authors can craft stories that resonate deeply, making readers feel as if they're journeying alongside real, living individuals.

Conclusion to section 2

In our storytelling universe, characters are the essential pillars. They're not just part of the story—they are the story's heartbeat, its very essence. We've walked through the complex process of building characters, understanding their minds, backgrounds, and what drives them. We've discussed how to represent cultures thoughtfully, maintain consistency, and create authentic characters.

Characters reflect our humanity—our hopes, fears, strengths, and weaknesses. They are like mirrors for readers, offering a glimpse into different lives and experiences. More than just reflections, well-crafted characters challenge and inspire us, becoming figures who guide us through the story's twists and turns.

As writers, we carry a significant responsibility. Our characters are more than just words on a page. They are a part of our legacy in the literary world. It's our job to shape them with careful attention, empathy, and depth, to ensure they resonate with readers on a deeper level. Whether they evoke laughter, tears, or contemplation, they should always leave an impact.

Ultimately, while an intriguing plot and an enchanting setting are important, it's the characters that truly capture readers' hearts. It's the characters they remember. They transform stories into living, breathing experiences. As we conclude this section, remember the importance of crafting your characters with care and precision. In fiction, characters are the vital link between the writer's imagination and the reader's heart. Create them thoughtfully, make them compelling, and let them lead your story to unforgettable places.

Section 3: Plotting & Pacing

> *"Research. Write. Repeat. This is your craft, treat it with the respect it deserves."*—**L. Marie Wood, Vice President of the Horror Writers Association and author of *The Realm Trilogy***

In every story that's stayed with us, from cozy campfire tales to epic novels, there's a pulse that keeps us hooked. That pulse? It's all about plotting and pacing. Think about the stories that have stayed with you. The emotional highs and lows, those edge-of-your-seat moments, and the deep satisfaction when everything ties up neatly—that's the power of a well-crafted plot and its pacing.

Plotting is like mapping out an exciting journey. It's planning the peaks and valleys, the sudden twists, and the moments that take your breath away. It's crafting the path you want your readers to follow, from the opening sentence to the final word. But remember, it's not just about the dramatic scenes; it's also about the quieter moments that give your readers a chance to breathe and reflect.

For those who love to 'pants' their way through stories (writing by the seat of their pants), the idea of plotting might seem a bit rigid. But even for pantsers, a touch of planning can be beneficial. Try a mix of both: maybe sketch out a rough ending, choose a starting point, and keep that ending in mind as you write. So don't be overwhelmed by all the information to come. See what balance works best for you.

Pacing, on the other hand, is the rhythm of your story. It's knowing when to speed things up, when to slowly build tension, and when to dive into action or emotion. It keeps your readers always on their toes, always craving what's next.

Together, plotting and pacing are the spine of your story. They decide if your reader will stay up all night, unable to stop reading, or if they'll lose interest. In this section, we'll delve into the art of plotting and pacing. We'll cover techniques, common mistakes, and tips to make sure your story keeps its readers captivated. So, get ready. We're about to start the thrilling journey of creating a story that pulses with life.

But... Before we get to Chapter 1, let's first discuss a vital aspect of great plotting. We've all been there: engrossed in a novel or movie, traveling through time or across continents, only to be jolted out of our immersion by a glaring inaccuracy. Maybe it's a character in ancient Rome munching on a potato (which wasn't introduced to Europe until much later) or a supposed "local" dialogue that sounds nothing like the real thing. These moments underscore the importance of research and authenticity in storytelling.

Why Research Matters:

- Readers or viewers come to a story willing to suspend disbelief, but they also trust the writer to guide them accurately through unfamiliar terrains. When details are right, that trust deepens. When they're wrong, it can be broken.

- Authentic details, whether it's the layout of a city, the nuances of a dialect, or the intricacies of a historical event, add layers of depth to a narrative. They make the world feel lived-in, real, and tangible.

- Proper research helps writers portray cultures, places, and times with nuance and respect, avoiding broad strokes or clichéd representations.

How to Dive In:
- Books and Articles: Start with the basics. History books, travel guides, academic articles, and firsthand accounts can provide a solid foundation. Don't just skim the surface; delve deep into the specifics of the time or place you're portraying.

- Expert Consultations: If you're writing about a specific profession, cultural practice, or historical event, consider consulting with an expert. Their insights can add layers of authenticity to your narrative.

- Travel, If Possible: If your story is set in a real-world location, visiting can provide invaluable insights. Feel the texture of the cobblestones, soak in the local ambiance, and chat with the locals. There's no substitute for firsthand experience.

- Multimedia Resources: Documentaries, podcasts, and even period-specific music or art can immerse you in the atmosphere of the setting or era you're exploring.

- Feedback from Sensitivity Readers: Especially when dealing with cultures or experiences outside your own, sensitivity readers can help ensure that your portrayal is respectful and accurate.

- The Balancing Act: While striving for accuracy, it's also essential to remember that you're crafting a narrative, not a textbook. The details should serve the story, adding authenticity without overwhelming the plot or characters. It's a delicate balance, but when struck right, the results are magical: a world that feels both wondrously new and deeply real.

Research isn't just a box to tick off; it's a bridge to authenticity. It's the writer's commitment to honoring the realities they're drawing from, ensuring that their tales resonate with both truth and heart. After all, in the words of the great Mark Twain, "Truth is stranger than fiction," and sometimes, diving into the real world can lead to the most compelling stories of all.

Chapter 1

Plot Structures

Every story, whether whispered around a campfire or sprawled across the pages of a bestseller, follows an invisible blueprint. This blueprint, or plot structure, is the skeleton upon which the flesh of characters, settings, and themes are layered. It's the guiding force that ensures a narrative flows smoothly, compellingly, and cohesively from beginning to end. And while there are countless ways to tell a tale, certain plot structures have stood the test of time, proving their worth again and again. Let's delve into some of these classic structures and understand their magic.

The Three-Act Structure:

Often likened to the beginning, middle, and end of a story, this structure is as old as storytelling itself.

Act 1 - The Opening Act: This is where your story begins, inviting readers into the world you've created. It's crucial to introduce the key players, your main characters, and give a glimpse into their lives and personalities. Here, you also set up the central conflict or problem that will drive the story. This act is about laying the groundwork, providing context, and creating intrigue that hooks your readers. It's the part where the setting is established, whether it's a bustling city or a quiet village, and where initial relationships and dynamics are explored.

Act 2 - The Heart of the Story: Act 2 is where the action heats up. It's typically the longest section of your narrative, where your characters are put through a series of challenges and obstacles. This act is crucial for character development; as they confront these challenges, they evolve, revealing strengths and weaknesses. The tension builds steadily here, leading to significant turning points or plot twists. This act is all about maintaining momentum, keeping your readers engaged with a mix of action, emotion, and discovery. Unfortunately Act 2 tends to be the hardest to write.

Act 3 - The Climactic Finale: In the final act, all the built-up tension and narrative threads come together. This is where the main conflict reaches its climax, often leading to a decisive confrontation or a significant revelation. The climax should be the most intense part of your story, where stakes are highest. Following this, the story moves toward its resolution, tying up loose ends and answering key questions. The ending might be triumphant, tragic, or bittersweet, but it should feel satisfying and fitting for the journey your characters and readers have been on.

The Hero's Journey:

You're about to take a journey following the footsteps of countless heroes before you, a path laid out by Joseph Campbell in *The Hero with a Thousand Faces*. It's a big, adventurous circle. Your character starts in their normal, everyday world, then gets pulled into an extraordinary adventure full of unknowns. They'll face challenges, change in big ways, and then come back home, but they won't be the same person they were when they left.

- Ordinary World: This is where we first meet our hero, just doing their usual thing. It's like the calm before the storm, showing us what their life was like before everything turned upside down.

- Call to Adventure: Something happens that shakes up the hero's world. It's the nudge (or sometimes a push) that sets them on their path.

- Crossing the Threshold: Here's where the hero says, "Okay, I'm doing this." They step into the adventure, leaving their old world behind.

- Trials and Challenges: The hero faces a bunch of challenges that test them and help them grow.

- The Climax: This is the big showdown, the hardest part of the journey where the hero faces their biggest challenge.

- Return: The hero comes back home, but they're not who they used to be. They've changed, learned something valuable, or maybe they've even got some treasure (either real or metaphorical).

These steps in The Hero's Journey are more than just plot points; they're a map for your storytelling adventure. They give your story a heartbeat, a rhythm, and a direction. But here's the thing: they're flexible. You can twist, turn, and play with them to make your story uniquely yours. They're guidelines, not strict rules. So go ahead, mix things up, and create a story that's all your own.

The Five-Act Structure

Ah, the Five-Act Structure! When we think of grand theaters, poetic dialogues, and the timeless tales of Shakespeare, this is the structure that often comes to mind. It's like a five-course meal, each act serving a distinct flavor, leading to a satisfying conclusion.

Originating from classical drama, the Five-Act Structure has been a cornerstone of storytelling for centuries. And while it might sound a bit formal, it's actually quite intuitive. Let's break it down:

1. Introduction: This is where we set the stage. Imagine entering a room and getting the lay of the land. Who's in the room? What's the vibe? In storytelling terms, we're introduced to the main characters, the setting, and the initial situation. It's like the appetizer of our five-course meal, giving us a taste of what's to come.

2. Rising Action: The plot thickens, tensions rise, and characters face challenges. It's the part of the story where you lean in a little closer, eager to see what happens next. If our story were a dance, this would be the part where the tempo picks up, and the dancers' movements become more intricate.

3. Climax: The big moment! All the tension, all the build-up, it all comes to a head here. It's the most intense part of the story, where the main conflict reaches its peak.

4. Falling Action: After the intensity of the climax, things start to wind down. The immediate conflicts are resolved, and the story begins its descent to a conclusion. It's like the cool-down after an intense workout, giving both the characters and the readers a moment to catch their breath.

5. Denouement: French for "untying," this is where all the loose ends are tied up. Questions are answered, mysteries are solved, and the story comes to a natural close. It's the dessert of our meal, a sweet ending to a rich and fulfilling experience.

The beauty of the Five-Act Structure is its versatility. While it has its roots in classical drama, it's been used in everything from epic novels to modern movies. It provides a clear roadmap for storytellers, ensuring that the narrative has a rhythm, a pulse, and a satisfying arc. So, the next time you're watching a Shakespeare play or reading a classic novel, see if you can spot this age-old structure in action. It's a testament to its enduring appeal that it continues to resonate with audiences, even today.

Freytag's Pyramid:

Ever thought of stories as a journey up and down a mountain? That's one way to think about Freytag's Pyramid. Named after Gustav Freytag, a 19th-century German playwright with a knack for analyzing drama, this structure gives us a visual guide to the ebb and flow of a story. It's like a mountain trek, where each stage has its own challenges and rewards.

Let's explore this pyramid:

- Exposition: This is the base camp of our mountain trek. Before we start our ascent, we need to know where we are and what's around us. In story terms, the exposition sets the scene. We meet the main characters, understand the setting, and get a hint of the conflicts to come. It's the calm before the storm, the moment of preparation before the adventure begins.

- Rising Action: As we start our climb, the path gets steeper and the challenges more intense. In the story, this is where conflicts start to escalate, obstacles appear, and tensions rise. Characters are tested, relationships evolve, and the stakes get higher. It's the heart-pounding part of the journey, where every step matters.

- Climax: We've reached the summit! This is the highest point of our trek, both literally and emotionally. In the narrative, the climax is where the main conflict reaches its peak. Decisions are made, battles are fought, and the fate of our characters hangs in the balance. It's the moment of truth, the turning point that determines how the story will end.

- Falling Action: After the adrenaline rush of the climax, we start our descent down the mountain. The immediate conflicts have been resolved, and the story starts to wind down. But there are still some loose rocks and slippery paths to navigate. In the narrative, this is where the consequences of the climax play out, leading us toward the story's conclusion.

- Denouement: We've made it back to base camp, safe and sound. It's time to reflect on our journey and see how far we've come. In the story, the denouement ties up any loose ends and brings the narrative to a satisfying close. It's the moment of resolution, where everything comes full circle.

Looks a lot like the five-act structure, right? This is a testament to the timeless nature of storytelling. While it was developed in the 19th century, its principles are still relevant today. Whether you're crafting a short story, a novel, or even a screenplay, this structure offers a clear and effective roadmap. It reminds us that stories, much like mountain treks, are about the journey as much as the destination. And with Freytag as our guide, we're in for a memorable adventure.

The Seven-Point Story Structure:

In the vast world of storytelling, there are countless ways to structure a narrative. Yet, amidst the myriad options, the Seven-Point Story Structure stands out, offering writers a clear roadmap to craft compelling tales. Popularized by the talented Dan Wells, this structure breaks down a story into seven pivotal moments, ensuring a rhythm that keeps readers hooked from start to finish.

- The Hook: Every great story begins with a promise, a moment that grabs the reader's attention and whispers, "This is a journey worth taking." The Hook is that initial intrigue, a scene or event that sets the tone and poses a question or challenge that the narrative will address.

- First Plot Point: As the story unfolds, it reaches a juncture where the protagonist's path becomes clear. This is the First Plot Point, a significant event or decision that propels the story forward, setting the main character on their journey.

- Pinch Point 1: Every tale needs its hurdles, moments that apply pressure on the protagonist, testing their resolve. The first Pinch Point introduces a challenge or antagonist, reminding readers of the stakes and the obstacles the hero must overcome.

- Midpoint: At the story's heart lies the Midpoint, a turning point where the protagonist gains a clearer understanding of their quest. It's a moment of reflection, realization, or a significant revelation that shifts the narrative's direction.

- Pinch Point 2: As the story progresses, the challenges intensify. The second Pinch Point ups the ante, presenting an even greater obstacle or threat, pushing the protagonist to their limits and setting the stage for the climax.

- Second Plot Point: As the narrative nears its climax, the Second Plot Point emerges. It's the final piece of information or event that the protagonist needs to begin their journey toward the resolution. It's the "all is lost" moment, where the stakes are highest, and the outcome seems uncertain.

- Resolution: Every journey, no matter how tumultuous, seeks an end. The Resolution provides closure, answering the questions posed by the Hook and showcasing the protagonist's growth or transformation.

You've probably realized that this structure is used in *a lot* of Hollywood movies. The beauty of the Seven-Point Story Structure lies in its simplicity and adaptability. Whether you're penning a heart-wrenching romance, a thrilling mystery, or an epic fantasy, these seven beats provide a framework that ensures pacing and progression. It's a dance of narrative moments, each step leading seamlessly to the next, guiding writers and readers through the captivating world of storytelling.

The "Save the Cat!" Beat Sheet:

When diving into the world of storytelling, especially in the realm of screenwriting, one name often pops up: Blake Snyder. His influential guide, *Save the Cat!*, has become a staple for many writers, offering a structured approach to crafting compelling narratives. I've read it countless times, and will probably need a new copy before I read it again. And I will. At the heart of Snyder's method is the Beat Sheet, a series of specific events or moments that a story should navigate, ensuring it resonates with audiences and maintains a rhythmic flow.

Let's delve into this cinematic storytelling approach:

1. Opening Image: Every story starts with a snapshot, a scene that sets the tone and introduces the world and its primary theme. It's the first impression, and as they say, it counts.
2. Theme Stated: Early on, the story's central theme or message is hinted at,

often subtly. It's a question or statement that the narrative will explore and answer.

3. Set-Up: Here, the main characters, their world, and their desires are introduced. It's the foundation upon which the rest of the story is built.

4. Catalyst: Every narrative needs a spark, an event that sets the protagonist on their journey. You've most likely gotten to know this as the Inciting Incident. It is that moment that shakes up the character's world and propels them into the unknown.

5. Debate: With the journey set, the protagonist grapples with the decision to move forward. It's a moment of doubt, reflection, and internal conflict, building anticipation for the adventure ahead.

6. Break into Two: Taking the plunge, the protagonist commits to their journey, marking a clear shift from the story's beginning to its middle.

7. B Story: A subplot or secondary story kicks off, often introducing new characters and themes that will support or contrast the main narrative.

8. Fun and Games: As the title suggests, this is where the story lets loose. It's a series of scenes showcasing the protagonist's adventures, challenges, and growth, often with a lighter tone.

9. Midpoint: The story's center is marked by a significant event, either a major success or a crushing setback for the protagonist. It's a turning point that raises the stakes and propels the narrative toward its climax.

10. Bad Guys Close In: Challenges intensify as antagonists, obstacles, and internal doubts converge on the protagonist, testing their resolve.

11. All Is Lost: The narrative's lowest point, where everything seems bleak and the protagonist's goals appear unreachable.

12. Dark Night of the Soul: A moment of introspection and despair, where the protagonist reflects on their journey, their failures, and the lessons learned.

13. Break into Three: Reinvigorated and armed with newfound insight, the protagonist decides to tackle their challenges head-on, marking the story's shift into its final act.

14. Finale: The climax, where all narrative threads converge, conflicts are resolved, and the protagonist faces their ultimate challenge.
15. Final Image: The story comes full circle with a closing snapshot, mirroring the opening image but showcasing the changes and growth that have occurred.

Blake Snyder's Save the Cat! Beat Sheet is more than just a formula—it's a guide to crafting stories that resonate, entertain, and linger in audiences' minds. By hitting these beats, writers ensure their tales have rhythm, depth, and a cinematic quality that captivates from start to finish. Whether you're penning a screenplay or adapting the method for a novel, the Beat Sheet offers a roadmap to storytelling success.

The Snowflake Method:

Every snowflake begins as a tiny ice crystal, growing and expanding into a unique, intricate design. Similarly, a story can start with a simple idea and, with careful nurturing, evolve into a rich, layered narrative. Enter the Snowflake Method, a brainchild of Randy Ingermanson. This approach to storytelling mirrors the formation of a snowflake, starting with a core concept and expanding it step by step until a full-fledged tale emerges.

Let's break down this fascinating approach to story crafting:

1. The Core Idea: Just as a snowflake starts with a single ice crystal, your story begins with a one-sentence summary. This sentence captures the essence of your tale, giving you a clear direction.
2. Expanding the Idea: From that initial sentence, you'll expand it into a full paragraph, outlining the story's major events, especially the beginning, middle, and end. It's like watching the ice crystal grow, branching out in different directions.

3. Characters Take the Stage: Now, it's time to dive into your story's players. For each major character, you'll craft a one-page summary detailing their motivations, goals, conflicts, and arcs. As you delve into their psyche, the narrative's shape becomes clearer, much like the intricate patterns of a snowflake forming.

4. Expanding the Plot: With characters in place, you'll return to the plot, expanding each sentence of your initial paragraph into a full paragraph of its own. This gives you a more detailed roadmap of your story's progression.

5. Deep Dive into Characters: Now, you'll craft detailed character charts, diving deeper into their backgrounds, relationships, and personal journeys. This step adds depth and dimension to your narrative, ensuring your characters are as multifaceted as a snowflake's design.

6. Expanding Scenes: Taking your four-paragraph summary, you'll list out every scene required to bring those paragraphs to life. This step-by-step breakdown ensures no detail is overlooked.

7. Detailed Scene Descriptions: Each scene gets a paragraph of its own, diving into the specifics. Who's involved? What's the setting? What conflicts arise? This is where the meat of your story starts to take shape.

8. The First Draft: With a comprehensive scene list in hand, you'll begin writing your first draft. Like a snowflake solidifying, your story comes to life, building on the foundation you've meticulously crafted.

9. Refinement: Just as nature refines each snowflake into a unique masterpiece, you'll refine your draft, tweaking and polishing until it shines.

10. Final Touches: With the bulk of the work done, you'll add the finishing touches, ensuring every element of your story aligns with your vision.

The beauty of the Snowflake Method lies in its structured yet organic approach. By starting small and building outward, writers ensure their stories are cohesive, detailed, and, most importantly, engaging. It's a testament to the power of gradual expansion, proving that even the most complex tales can grow from the simplest of ideas. So, the next time you're daunted by the blank page, remember the humble snowflake and let your story unfold, one step at a time. I'd recommend this approach for someone attempting a novel for the very first time.

The M.I.C.E. Quotient

Orson Scott Card's M.I.C.E. Quotient is a unique framework of breaking down and building stories. It's all about understanding four key elements: Milieu, Idea, Character, and Event. Each one plays a different role in shaping a story.

- Milieu: This part focuses on the story's setting or world. In a milieu-driven story, it's all about the world itself and exploring it. Think of *The Lord of the Rings* where Middle-earth isn't just a backdrop, but a character in its own right. These stories start when the character enters a new world and end when they leave it.

- Idea: Here, the story is built around a central question or problem. It starts when this question is posed and ends when it's answered. Mystery novels often follow this pattern, revolving around solving a crime or uncovering a secret.

- Character: Character-driven stories zoom in on the personal journey of a character. These narratives begin with a character's dissatisfaction or struggle and end with their transformation or resolution. A classic example is *The Great Gatsby*, focusing on Jay Gatsby's personal evolution and ultimate fate.

- Event: These stories are about setting the world right after something goes wrong. They start with a disruptive event and end when order is restored or a new balance is found. Many adventure and hero stories fit this mold, focusing on overcoming challenges and resolving conflicts.

The M.I.C.E. Quotient isn't just for dissecting stories, though. It's great for crafting them, too. It helps writers figure out what's at the heart of their story and keep their narrative focused and engaging. And these elements often mix and match, adding layers to the story. For example, a tale might begin focused on a character but evolve to include significant milieu or idea elements.

A few smaller plot devices:

In storytelling, various plotting methods offer unique ways to structure narratives. **The Mirror Structure** is one such method where the second half of the story reflects the first half, often used in tales featuring a journey that leads out and then back. **In Medias Res** is another technique, originating from the Latin phrase meaning "into the middle of things." It starts the story in the midst of action, with flashbacks or other devices providing the backstory later. The **Nonlinear Structure** breaks away from chronological storytelling, instead jumping back and forth in time. This approach can build suspense and offer more profound insights into characters and events. Lastly, the **Circular Structure** brings the story back to where it began, creating a sense of completeness or suggesting a continuous cycle. Each of these methods provides a different lens through which a story can be told, enriching the narrative and engaging readers in various and often unexpected ways.

Chapter 2

The importance of a strong beginning, middle, and end.

A good plot is like a path through an uncharted forest. It's your job to clear the way for your readers.

In the craft of storytelling, every compelling tale hinges on three essential elements: a gripping beginning, a dynamic middle, and a fulfilling end. Each of these segments plays a crucial role in shaping a narrative that resonates deeply with readers.

The Beginning: Capturing the Reader's Imagination

The beginning of a story is where the magic starts. It's the crucial moment that pulls readers into the world you've created. This is where you introduce the key characters, set the scene, and present the central premise of your story. More importantly, a strong beginning should hook the reader with an intriguing problem, question, or scenario, compelling them to turn the page. It's about setting the tone and sparking curiosity right from the start.

The Middle: Keeping the Momentum

As the story progresses into the middle, this is where the plot deepens and characters are further developed. It's the heart of the story, where the initial setups begin to evolve, conflicts intensify, and characters are pushed to their limits. This part of the story needs to maintain engagement, driving the narrative forward with escalating events or unfolding mysteries that keep readers invested and eager to see what happens next.

The End: Delivering a Satisfying Conclusion

The conclusion of a story is where all threads come together. A well-executed ending resolves the central conflicts and addresses the key questions posed throughout the story. It should provide a sense of closure, leaving the reader with a feeling of satisfaction, regardless of whether the ending is happy, sad, or open-ended. The goal is to make a lasting impact, leaving readers to ponder the story long after they've finished reading.

Integrating the Three Elements

Though the beginning, middle, and end each serve distinct purposes, they are interconnected. An effective beginning sets the stage for a middle that expands on the story's themes and character arcs, leading seamlessly into an ending that feels both earned and rewarding. The smooth transition and coherence among these three parts are what make a story feel complete and unified, providing a truly immersive reading experience.

Chapter 3

Character-Driven vs. Plot-Driven Stories

In storytelling, two primary narrative approaches shape the journey of a tale: character-driven and plot-driven stories. Recognizing their differences and deciding which best suits your story can greatly impact its development and the experience it offers to readers.

Character-Driven Stories:

Character-driven stories place the spotlight on the internal journey of the characters, exploring their emotional evolution, motivations, and personal transformations. These narratives delve deep into the complexities of their personalities, relationships, and life choices. The plot in such stories typically unfolds in response to the characters' actions and decisions, making their inner development and change the heart of the story. The effectiveness of these stories hinges on the depth and authenticity of the character development. A great example is *The Girl with All the Gifts* by M.R. Carey, where a deep exploration of the main character significantly drives the plot.

Plot-Driven Stories:

Conversely, plot-driven stories focus on the sequence of events and the external action that propels the narrative. In these stories, the plot acts as the main driver, with characters often playing roles that serve the progression of events. Such stories are usually fast-paced, characterized by a series of events and conflicts that keep the story moving. The emphasis is more on what happens rather than on who it happens to. Thrillers and mystery novels often fall into this category, where the unfolding of events is central to the narrative. A perfect example is Josh Malerman's *Bird Box*. Although we spend a lot of time with Malorie, it's a series of events and external conflicts that drive the story forward. It's not just happening to her. It's happening to everyone.

Choosing the Right Approach for Your Story

The choice between a character-driven or plot-driven approach depends on the type of story you intend to tell and the impact you wish to have on your audience. If your aim is to explore the inner workings of your characters, a character-driven story may be more fitting. However, if your focus is on crafting an action-packed narrative where the sequence of events takes precedence, then a plot-driven approach might be more appropriate.

Both character-driven and plot-driven stories offer distinct pathways to captivate readers, each with its own strengths. By understanding these two approaches and choosing the one that aligns with your storytelling goals, you can enhance the impact and appeal of your narrative, ensuring it resonates deeply with your audience.

Chapter 4

Conflict and Tension

In the heart of every compelling story lies conflict and tension, the dynamic elements that keep readers hooked and drive the narrative forward. Whether it's a spine-chilling horror tale, a thrilling mystery, or a heartfelt drama, conflict is the engine that powers the plot and engages the audience.

Conflict:

At its core, conflict is a clash of opposing forces, and it comes in many forms. It could be internal, where characters struggle with their own beliefs, desires, or fears, or external, involving other characters clashing (opposite personalities rubbing each other the wrong way or two alphas competing for leadership), societal norms, or even nature itself. It's this conflict that creates a compelling reason for the story to unfold. Without it, there's little to propel characters into action or to challenge them, and consequently, little to captivate the reader. Conflict *is* the driving force of plot.

In horror stories, conflict often arises from a character's encounter with the supernatural or their struggle against an incomprehensible evil. This not only moves the plot but also creates an atmosphere of suspense and dread, essential in horror writing.

Tension:

Tension, on the other hand, is the sense of anticipation and anxiety that builds up as the conflict unfolds. It's what keeps readers turning the pages, eager to see how the characters will navigate their challenges. Tension can be subtle, a quiet sense of unease, or it can be overt, with high-stakes and fast-paced action. It keeps the reader engaged.

In crafting tension, the key is to balance the elements of surprise and suspense. It's about knowing when to reveal information and when to hold back, keeping the reader guessing. Tension is often most effective when it's drawn out, allowing the reader's anticipation to build before reaching a climax.

Conflict and tension are indispensable in storytelling. They are the elements that give a story its rhythm and pulse. By skillfully weaving conflict into the narrative and managing tension to keep the audience engaged, writers can create stories that are not only captivating and entertaining but also resonate emotionally with readers. Whether it's a battle against a terrifying monster, a struggle with inner demons, or a conflict with a formidable adversary, it's these challenges and the tension they bring that make a story truly memorable.

Different types of conflict:

Conflict is the cornerstone of storytelling, providing the necessary tension and energy that keeps a narrative engaging. It comes in various forms, each serving a unique purpose in developing the plot and characters. Understanding these different types of conflict is crucial for any writer aiming to craft a compelling story.

Internal Conflict:

Internal conflict occurs within a character, involving struggles of the mind, emotions, or conscience. This type of conflict is about the character battling their own fears, desires, or ethical dilemmas. It's a deeply personal journey that often drives character development. For example, a protagonist may grapple with guilt, self-doubt, or a moral choice, creating a complex and relatable character journey.

External Conflict:

External conflict involves a character facing obstacles in the external world. This could be a physical struggle against other characters, nature, or societal structures. External conflicts are often easier to visualize and can range from simple scenarios like a survival challenge in the wilderness to complex societal issues like war or oppression.

Interpersonal Conflict:

Interpersonal conflict arises between characters due to differences in goals, beliefs, or personalities. This type of conflict is integral to developing relationships within the story. It could manifest as rivalry, misunderstanding, or ideological differences, providing a platform for dialogue and interaction that adds depth to the narrative.

Other Forms of Conflict:

Beyond these basic types, conflict can also manifest in other ways, such as cultural or ideological conflicts, where characters must navigate differing worldviews or societal norms. Technological or supernatural conflicts are also common in certain genres, where characters face challenges beyond the ordinary.

The different types of conflict are essential tools in a writer's arsenal. They add complexity, depth, and realism to a story, driving both plot and character development. Whether it's the inner turmoil of a character, their struggle against an external force, the friction between characters, or other forms of conflict, each contributes to the rich tapestry of the narrative. By skillfully integrating these various forms of conflict, writers can create stories that are not just engaging and entertaining but also reflective of the multifaceted nature of human experience.

> The only way to silence self-doubt is to write. Each word you pen is a battle won against fear.

Chapter 5
Pacing and Rhythm

Pacing and rhythm are critical elements in storytelling, dictating the flow and engagement of a narrative. A well-paced story keeps readers invested from start to finish, skillfully balancing high-energy action with reflective, slower moments. Understanding and controlling the pace of a story is crucial for creating an absorbing and well-rounded narrative.

The Dance of Pacing

The essence of good pacing lies in its variability. Fast-paced scenes, often brimming with action and dialogue, drive the story forward, creating a sense of urgency and excitement. These scenes are crucial for keeping readers' adrenaline pumping and ensuring that the story maintains its momentum. However, constantly operating at this intensity can overwhelm the reader, leaving little room for character development or thematic exploration.

To counter this, slower, more introspective moments are necessary. These scenes allow for character reflection, world-building, and the exploration of themes and relationships. They provide readers with a chance to breathe, absorb, and reflect on the events of the story. This balance between action and introspection is key to creating a rhythm that feels natural and engaging.

Techniques to Control Pacing

- The length and structure of sentences can significantly affect pacing. Short, choppy sentences can quicken the pace, ideal for action sequences or tense moments. Conversely, longer, more complex sentences tend to slow down the narrative, suitable for moments of reflection or detailed descriptions.

- How a chapter ends can also influence pacing. Ending a chapter with a cliffhanger or an unresolved issue can propel the reader to continue, maintaining the story's momentum. Strategic chapter breaks can provide natural pauses in the narrative, giving readers time to process the story before plunging into the next segment.

- Rapid-fire dialogue can accelerate pacing, while descriptive passages can slow it down. Balancing dialogue and description based on the needs of the scene can help control the story's tempo.

- Changing the point of view can also impact pacing. Switching between characters or perspectives can either quicken the pace by introducing new, immediate conflicts or slow it down to explore different aspects of the story.

- The structure of the plot itself influences pacing. A series of escalating events can quicken the pace, while a more meandering plot might slow it down. It's important to consider how each plot point contributes to the overall pacing of the story.

- Different genres often have different pacing expectations. For instance, thrillers tend to have a faster pace than literary fiction. Understanding genre conventions can help in tailoring the pacing to meet readers' expectations.

Mastering pacing and rhythm is akin to conducting a symphony. It requires an understanding of when to speed up the tempo and when to slow it down. The goal is to create a narrative that flows naturally, capturing the reader's interest throughout and providing a satisfying reading experience. Whether through the rapid currents of action or the gentle streams of introspection, pacing is the heartbeat of a story, vital in bringing the narrative to life.

Chapter 6
Subplots and Side Stories

In the craft of horror storytelling, subplots and side stories are akin to the intricate layers that add depth and dimension to the main narrative. They're the essential secondary threads that, when skillfully intertwined with the primary plot, enrich the story with complexity and realism. For writers, mastering the integration of these elements is key to creating a narrative that's both engaging and resonant.

Integrating Secondary Narratives: The art of including subplots involves ensuring they complement or contrast the main story in meaningful ways. A good subplot is like a supporting character that enhances the main plot, offering fresh perspectives or shedding light on various aspects of the story or characters. It should feel like an integral part of the narrative tapestry, intersecting with the main plot at critical points and contributing to the story's depth.

You might use a subplot to delve into a character's backstory, enriching their motivations and actions in the main plot. Alternatively, a subplot might run parallel to the main story, converging at key moments to heighten the drama or tension.

Subplots in Character Development and Theme Exploration: Subplots can be a powerful tool for exploring the nuances of characters' personalities and relationships. By placing characters in diverse situations or combining different character dynamics in subplots, writers can reveal various facets of their personalities and growth.

Additionally, subplots offer a more subtle avenue for exploring themes or social issues. They can act as a backdrop that reflects or contrasts the larger themes of the main plot, adding layers of meaning and depth to the narrative.

Maintaining Focus: While subplots enrich a story, it's important to keep the main plot in sharp focus. Subplots should enhance, not overshadow, the primary narrative. This balance is achieved by ensuring each subplot is tightly connected to the main plot, either through characters, themes, or events. Concluding these subplots in a way that contributes to the overall narrative arc is also vital for a cohesive story.

When effectively integrated, subplots amplify the main plot, deepen character development, and enrich thematic exploration. The skill lies in weaving these secondary narratives harmoniously with the main plot, crafting a story that is cohesive, captivating, and rich with meaning.

Chapter 7
Foreshadowing

Mastering Foreshadowing and Planting Information in Storytelling

In the art of storytelling, foreshadowing and the strategic placement of information are essential techniques for creating a layered and compelling narrative. These elements serve to hint at future events, creating suspense and keeping readers engaged. However, striking the right balance between being too subtle and too obvious is a delicate art that requires skill and finesse.

Foreshadowing: Foreshadowing is the technique of dropping subtle hints about plot developments that will occur later in the story. This can be done in various ways: through dialogue, descriptions, symbols, or events that mirror or suggest future happenings. The key is to plant these hints in a way that they are not immediately obvious but become meaningful in hindsight.

Effective foreshadowing creates a sense of anticipation and curiosity in the reader. It's like leaving a trail of breadcrumbs that readers can follow, building up to a larger, often surprising, revelation. For example, an offhand comment made by a character might later reveal a significant plot twist, or a seemingly random event might set the stage for a crucial storyline.

Balancing Subtlety and Obviousness: The challenge in using foreshadowing is in the balance. If it's too subtle, readers might miss the hints completely, rendering them ineffective. On the other hand, if it's too obvious, it can spoil the surprise and reduce the impact of the revelation. The goal is to leave enough clues to pique readers' interest without giving away the plot.

One approach to achieving this balance is to weave the foreshadowing seamlessly into the narrative so that it feels like a natural part of the story. Another method is to use misdirection, where some hints are designed to lead the reader to false conclusions, thereby enhancing the impact of the actual outcome.

Laying the Groundwork: Closely related to foreshadowing is the technique of planting information. This involves strategically placing key pieces of information throughout the narrative that are crucial for the understanding of later events. This could be background information, character details, or elements of the story world.

The successful planting of information ensures that when major plot points or twists occur, they feel earned and believable. It allows the story to unfold in a way that feels organic and ensures that the narrative progression makes sense.

Foreshadowing and planting information are techniques that can greatly enhance the suspense and depth of a story. They involve careful planning and a keen understanding of the narrative's trajectory. By mastering these techniques, writers can craft stories that not only captivate and intrigue readers but also provide a satisfying and cohesive reading experience. The key lies in the subtle art of hinting without revealing, building anticipation while keeping the reader guessing until the crucial moments of revelation. But don't let this distract you too much while you're writing your first draft. You can always add these in your second or third rewrite or during the editing stage.

"A word after a word after a word is power."—**Margaret Atwood**

Chapter 8
Flashbacks

Time jumps and non-chronological storytelling are powerful narrative techniques that can add depth and intrigue to a story. These methods involve moving back and forth in time or revealing events out of their chronological order. However, the challenge lies in executing these techniques without confusing the reader, and in using them to enhance rather than detract from the narrative.

Effective Use of Time Jumps: Time jumps can be a great way to reveal key background information, show character development over time, or create suspense. The key to using time jumps effectively is clarity. It's crucial for readers to understand when the jump is happening and where in the timeline the story has moved. This can be achieved through clear markers in the text, such as dates, explicit references to past events, or distinctive shifts in the narrative voice or style.

Another important aspect is ensuring that each time period is sufficiently developed. Time jumps should serve a purpose, whether it's to provide crucial backstory, reveal character growth, or set up future events. Each segment of the story, regardless of when it occurs chronologically, should contribute to the overall narrative and character arcs.

Impact of Revealing Information Out of Order: Presenting events out of their traditional chronological order can create a sense of mystery and compel readers to piece together the story. This technique can be used to gradually reveal information, keeping readers engaged as they try to understand the full picture. It can also add emotional depth, as past events are often revealed in light of their impact on the present.

However, this approach requires careful planning to ensure the narrative remains coherent and the revelations are impactful. The writer must judiciously decide what information to withhold and when to reveal it. The challenge is to maintain a balance between keeping the reader intrigued and avoiding unnecessary confusion. This is a skill that requires practice and a lot of reading. Next time you read a book, highlight these moments and ask yourself why the author decided to place them at those specific points.

When used thoughtfully, flashback can enhance the storytelling by deepening character development, enriching the plot, and engaging the reader in an active role of piecing together the narrative puzzle. The success of these techniques lies in their clarity, purposefulness, and impact on the overall narrative.

Chapter 9
Climax and Resolution

In the architecture of a story—especially horror—the climax and resolution are pivotal elements that determine its overall impact and effectiveness. The climax is the high point of tension and conflict, while the resolution is where the story's loose ends are tied up, providing closure. Mastering these elements is crucial for a fulfilling storytelling experience.

Crafting a Satisfying Climax: The climax in horror is where the main conflict escalates to its most intense point. It's the culmination of all the eerie tension and drama built up throughout the story. A strong climax often involves a final, nail-biting confrontation or a crucial decision that pushes the protagonist to their limit. This pivotal scene should be a natural and inevitable result of the events and character decisions leading up to it, ensuring that it feels earned and believable.

In creating an impactful climax, it's important to raise the stakes and increase the tension to the maximum. The climax should challenge the protagonist in unexpected ways, pushing them to make significant choices or sacrifices. This not only adds to the drama but also facilitates character growth, making the climax both thrilling and meaningful.

The Importance of Resolution and Closure: Following the climax, the resolution is where the story's remaining questions are answered and conflicts are resolved. This part is essential for providing a sense of closure to the story and its characters. A satisfying resolution ties up the story's loose ends, resolving subplots and character arcs in a way that aligns with the story's themes and the journey of the characters.

The resolution should leave the reader with a clear understanding of the outcomes for the characters and the world of the story. It's also an opportunity to reflect on the themes explored and the journey undertaken, giving the reader a sense of completion and fulfillment.

In some stories, the resolution may leave room for interpretation or set the stage for future narratives, but even in these cases, it should provide enough closure to be satisfying.

The climax and resolution are the heart and soul of a story. The climax is where the narrative tension reaches its zenith, delivering the emotional and dramatic payoff that the story has been building towards. The resolution then provides the necessary closure, answering the lingering questions and solidifying the characters' journeys. Together, they form the emotional core of the narrative, leaving a lasting impression on the reader.

Chapter 10
Twists and Surprises

The art of crafting twists and surprises can be likened to a magician's most captivating trick. For horror authors, executing these elements skillfully can turn a story into an unforgettable experience, startling and enthralling readers. The effectiveness of twists lies in their ability to be both unforeseen yet completely logical within the context of the eerie world you've created.

Crafting Unexpected Plot Turns: A successful twist in a story should catch the reader off guard while fitting perfectly into the narrative's logic. To pull this off, an author needs to lay a groundwork where the twist is possible but not immediately apparent. This often means planting subtle hints or clues throughout the story, enough to support the twist but not so overt as to give it away too soon.

In a horror story, misdirection plays a crucial role. You might lead readers to expect a typical ghost story, only to reveal a more psychological horror rooted in the protagonist's mind. Red herrings and misdirecting focus away from vital details are key techniques in this regard.

Another approach involves crafting multi-dimensional characters whose complex motivations and actions lead to unexpected but plausible plot developments. In horror, where characters often face extreme situations, their surprising decisions can pivot the entire story.

Ensuring Believability and Consistency: For a twist in a horror tale to be impactful, it must align with the established rules of the story's universe and the characters within it. It should feel like a natural part of the tale, not just a shock for shock's sake. The twist not only elevates the horror but also deepens the reader's understanding of the story or the characters involved.

The groundwork for a believable twist includes the previously mentioned subtle clues, woven seamlessly into the story. When the twist hits, readers should experience a jolt of surprise, quickly followed by the realization that the story was building up to this moment all along.

Creating effective twists and surprises is a nuanced and intricate task. It demands meticulous planning, a keen eye for detail, and a deep understanding of how to steer and then upend reader expectations. A well-crafted twist can elevate a horror story from the ordinary to the extraordinary, making it both more engaging and thought-provoking. Mastering this aspect of storytelling is a testament to an author's narrative skill and significantly enhances the reader's experience, making the horror story linger in their mind long after the last page is turned.

Chapter 11
Theme and Message

In storytelling, weaving theme and message into the plot transforms a simple story into a profound experience. The theme is the deeper meaning or insight into life that the story conveys, and how this is integrated into the plot can significantly elevate the narrative's impact.

Conveying Deeper Messages in Horror Plots: A well-crafted plot in horror does more than just scare or entertain. It acts as a vehicle for deeper messages and exploration of universal themes. Horror stories can address themes ranging from existential dread to societal issues, all while delivering the chills and thrills. The art lies in integrating these themes seamlessly into the plot, allowing them to naturally arise from the characters' experiences and choices.

For instance, in a horror story, the protagonist's journey through terrifying situations can reflect broader themes like survival, morality, or the struggle against unseen forces, thus highlighting deeper aspects of the human psyche or societal fears.

Exploring Universal Themes: Themes in horror stories become universal when they resonate with common human experiences and emotions. A story about a haunted house, for example, might explore themes of grief or the past's hold on the present, making it relatable on a deeper level.

The exploration of themes in horror can also provoke thought and stir discussions, challenging readers to reflect on their beliefs and fears. This is achieved by presenting themes in a way that invites different interpretations and perspectives.

Integrating theme and message into the plot is essential in creating a compelling horror story. It's what gives the narrative its depth and enduring impact. By weaving these elements thoughtfully into the plot, a writer crafts a story that goes beyond mere entertainment to provide insights into life's complexities and the darker corners of human existence.

> *"Horror is usually considered a genre all about fear, but here's the thing: fears are not universal. What scares one person will not necessarily scare the next. Over the years, I've found as both an author and a reader that the most important thing is that an author is writing from their own heart and their own experience; if you bring your own fears to the page, that's what is most likely to resonate with your readers, because it's so honest and personal. So explore what frightens you, and work that into your writing; that way, you'll be sure to create stories that stick with your audience long after they've turned the final page."*—**Gwendolyn Kiste**

Chapter 12

Revising and Refining the Plot

The process of writing a story is only the beginning. It's in the revising and refining where a plot truly comes to life. This crucial phase involves evaluating and strengthening the narrative, ensuring that the plot is cohesive, engaging, and impactful. Mastering the art of revision is key to transforming a good story into a great one.

Evaluating the Plot: The first step in revising is to take a step back and critically evaluate the plot. This involves looking at the narrative structure as a whole to ensure it's coherent and compelling. Key questions to consider include: Does the plot flow logically? Are there any inconsistencies or plot holes? Does each scene move the story forward? This holistic view helps identify areas that need tightening or expansion.

Another important aspect of evaluation is pacing. Assess whether the story maintains a good balance between action and quieter moments, ensuring that the narrative doesn't rush or drag at any point.

Strengthening the Plot: Once the evaluation is done, the next step is to strengthen the plot. This can involve several techniques:

- Ensure that the central conflict is clear and compelling. Enhance tension where necessary to keep readers engaged.

- Look at how the characters evolve throughout the story. Strengthening character development can add depth to the plot.

- Make sure that subplots are well-integrated and contribute to the main narrative. Remove or rewrite any that detract from the overall story.

- Revisit the themes of your story. Ensure they are woven seamlessly into the plot and resonate clearly with the reader.

- Review dialogue and descriptions to ensure they're effective and efficient. Dialogue should sound natural and descriptions should paint a vivid picture without being overwrought.

- Sometimes, it's beneficial to get an external perspective. Feedback from beta readers or writing groups can provide valuable insights.

- Be prepared to go through several rounds of revisions. Each draft should refine and improve the plot, bringing you closer to your final, polished narrative.

Revising and refining the plot is a meticulous and critical part of the writing process. It involves careful analysis and strengthening of the narrative, ensuring that every element, from the plot structure to character arcs, works harmoniously to create a compelling story. This process of evaluation and refinement is where a writer's skills are truly honed, and it's what turns a rough draft into a polished, engaging, and memorable piece of literature. The revision process, while often challenging, is immensely rewarding.

Chapter 13

Signs and Wonders: Revising to help your reader navigate your world
by Kate Maruyama

Revision is teaching your reader the best way to read your book...

When I heard this at a genre conference, it contextualized everything I have taught the writers in my novel and short story workshops for years. When we start writing, we dream of a world that feels concrete in our heads. The world and characters are often completely visible to us, and as we tell their stories, we tell it as if it's a story about an old friend, "You know this guy." We are trying, in horror especially, to be subtle and careful not to reveal too much or to belabor our points. We weave our tale. But often, in our move to keep things mysterious, we leave our reader completely out of these machinations. We may completely visualize a character and their entire world, but without signposts along the way, our readers can find our stories hard to get a handle on, vague, or sometimes confusing.

I came up against this problem when I was revising my first horror novel, *Harrowgate*. It is the story of a man, Michael, whose wife, Sarah, and newborn child, Tim, are dead, but their ghosts are living with him in his apartment. He tries like hell to keep the world out so he can spend more time with them, but eventually their very real funeral comes about.

I had about the best editor a writer can ask for, but during the funeral, my editor's notes got crankier and crankier. We are wrapped up in Michael's thoughts during the funeral, and cut back to his wife's ghostly point of view as things get weird for her. The editor said *why are we spending so much time on this funeral???* To his credit the sequence is about thirty pages, but I couldn't understand his frustration. I realized something and I wrote an email back in all caps, *WAIT YOU DON'T KNOW THAT THERE IS A BATTLE FOR SARAH'S SOUL HERE???*

He did not.

This careful and close reader had completely missed the point of this super important climactic scene in the book. I thought I was being subtle, but actually I was just being obtuse. And what was on the page, he was so right, was an extensively long funeral, and a reception, and some vagueness going on back at the apartment with the ghost wife.

For my rewrite, I went through and put signposts throughout the scenes, letting the reader know the longer this funeral went on, the more likely Michael was to lose his wife. In each scene I layered in some *watch, this is important*, tiny sentences here and there. I never overtly said, *The more prayers the priest says over Sarah's soul, the more likely it is she will be gone when Michael goes home.* But there was enough there to ratchet up the tension and to put the reader in those fears, both in Sarah's scenes so we notice she is being pulled away from this plane, and in the funeral.

The trick, when we've revised and done drafts for all of the tools I share in my "Editing Your Own Work," class with the Crystal Lake Academy on Heartbeat, is to go through each scene in our books and make sure they have all the details and signposts a reader needs to navigate them. Slowly remind yourself of what your reader doesn't know yet. *I have this scene in here to lay the groundwork for the giant thing that happens later in the book. But what does a reader need to know about this scene?* Ask yourself if you need to add a few zingers or signposts to make sure the reader knows this scene is important on a larger level. Or if you need to slow down a description, to take an eerier closer look at something.

I tell my students, it's as if you stand behind the reader, your hand on their shoulder saying, "Watch this, this here is important, and look over here, pay attention to this." And this is done by slowing down or by putting in signposts. Think of whoever your narrator is and how they, through the close point of view of their character, notice what is going on. Pay attention to what seems important to them. You can slow down in a frightening moment to take an extra breath describing something terrifying. You may have a full gory ghoul in your head who is wearing jewelry that will come into play later, but unless you slow down in the description of this ghoul, or let the protagonist take an extra moment of observation, we won't know the treasure is important. *His protruding hand had a large, gold ring on it, its glitter put into stark relief by the gray of his skin.* Signposts don't have to be overt, *this ring will be important later,* but a few extra phrases, or breaths around an object or moment, can highlight something that can be seen as important later. What you are saying to your reader is *Look at this ring, it will come up again.* As readers, we realize, "Oh, we didn't have a description of that—gun, entryway to a castle, sword scabbard, can of gasoline—for nothing." We collect these moments and things almost like objects in a videogame.

You need signposts mostly in scenes that are not directly driving the story forward, but scenes that are there to lay the larger web of story you're weaving together. Find those scenes and sit in them for a moment; imagine you are coming to them for the very first time. Do you have all the information you need? Are you clearly communicating that your reader is still in a horror story?

You are the host of this story, make sure your reader is having the best time.

Conclusion to section 3

In wrapping up this section on plotting and pacing in horror writing, we've delved into the essentials of crafting a narrative that grips and terrifies readers. A well-planned plot and carefully measured pacing are the backbone of effective horror storytelling. They are the tools that guide the reader through the dark and twisted paths of your narrative, keeping them enthralled from the first page to the last.

Plotting in horror requires a balance between the expected and the unexpected, weaving together elements of suspense, surprise, and the macabre. Pacing, on the other hand, is the rhythm of your story, dictating when to quicken the heartbeat with tension and when to slow down for moments of creeping dread.

As you venture forward in your writing journey, remember that the mastery of plotting and pacing is a skill honed over time and with practice. Each story you craft is an opportunity to refine these skills. So, embrace the challenge, experiment with different techniques, and most importantly, trust your instincts as a horror writer. Your unique voice and approach to storytelling are what will ultimately make your work stand out in the chilling expanse of horror literature.

Section 4: Writer's Life

Chapter 1

The ups and downs of being an author

The life of an author is often romanticized, envisioned as a serene journey of crafting worlds and characters. However, the reality is a rollercoaster of emotional, physical, and social challenges, each demanding its own unique coping strategies.

Mental and Emotional Challenges

- Creative Pressure: Authors frequently face the daunting task of birthing original ideas and weaving them into compelling narratives. This creative pressure can lead to writer's block, where the fear of not being good enough or not producing anything worthwhile can be paralyzing.

- Coping with Rejection: Rejection is a constant companion for most authors. Whether it's a manuscript being turned down by publishers or negative reviews from readers, dealing with rejection requires a thick skin and an ability to separate personal worth from professional setbacks. Remember, you're not the one being judged, and even if a story is turned down, there are numerous reasons that only the publisher or editor are aware of.

- Isolation: Writing is often a solitary endeavor. Long hours spent alone can lead to feelings of isolation and disconnect from the outside world. This can be particularly challenging for those who thrive on social interaction.

- Emotional Rollercoaster: Writing can be an emotional journey. Authors often experience highs when the writing flows and lows when it doesn't. This emotional volatility can be draining and requires a balanced approach to mental health.

Physical Challenges

- Sedentary Lifestyle: The nature of writing demands long periods of sitting, which can lead to a sedentary lifestyle. This poses risks like obesity, cardiovascular issues, and muscle strain, especially from poor posture. This has been my biggest obstacle.

- Eye Strain: Staring at a computer screen for extended periods can cause significant eye strain, leading to headaches and vision problems.

Social Challenges

- Balancing Relationships: The time and energy demands of writing can strain personal relationships. Authors must balance their passion for writing with the needs of their family and friends.

- Networking and Public Speaking: Many authors, especially introverts, find the social aspects of their career, like networking and public speaking at events, to be challenging.

Coping Strategies

- Establishing a routine can help manage the unpredictability of the writing process. Discipline in writing, even when inspiration is lacking, is crucial.

- Incorporating physical activity into daily routines can counteract the sedentary nature of writing. Regular exercise not only improves physical health but also mental well-being.

- Engaging with a community of fellow writers can alleviate feelings of isolation and provide a support system for dealing with rejection and sharing successes. This is why I felt the need to create our Shadows & Ink community on Heartbeat.

- Seeking professional help for mental health issues is important. Therapists can provide strategies to cope with the emotional ups and downs of a writing career.

- Prioritizing work-life balance is essential. Allocating time for family, friends, and hobbies can provide a much-needed break from the writing world. Remember, being an author is a long-term endeavor. It's a marathon, not a sprint.

- Building resilience against rejection and criticism is key. Understanding that these are part of the process and not reflections of personal failure is crucial.

- Long hours of writing can take a toll on your body. Investing in an ergonomic workspace is not just about comfort—it's about your health. An ergonomic chair, a properly set-up desk, and regular breaks to stretch and move can prevent chronic pains and strains associated with writing. Avoid a future where every writing session is marred by pain. It's hard being creative when you're constantly distracted.

Remember, writing is not just about putting words on paper; it's about taking care of the writer, too. By adopting these coping strategies, you can navigate the ups and downs of a writing career with more ease and resilience.

Chapter 2

It's No Joke by Graham Masterton

Ever since I first started writing fiction (which was when I was knee high to a high knee) I have asked myself how I can involve my readers to the point where they almost believe that they are living in the worlds that I have created.

Of course there are many basic ways of doing this, such as simplicity of language, songlike rhythm, and the use of easily-understandable words.

In his novel *The Process*, my late friend Bryon Gysin said that a box of matches "chuckles" when shaken. In other novels, I have read that when rain started to fall on hedges, they "crackled, as if they were on fire." Another author, whose name I regretfully forget, talks about a "laundering wind that bares your bones." (I did try to look this up on Google, but all I found were articles about the Mafia in Italy using wind farms to launder drugs money).

William Burroughs and I used to spend hours discussing ways of making books come alive. We agreed that it was important when you write not just to have your attention fixed on the page in front of you but to be aware of what your characters can hear and feel and smell. The wind blowing against the back of your neck, the smell of smoke drifting across the garden, the sound of a distant ship hooting in the harbour. William used to say "Pick up your typewriter and walk."

But I have also found that my lifelong interest in music-hall comedians was extremely helpful in writing stories that made my readers feel involved.

Music-hall comedians would often spend years travelling around the country playing to some of the most cynical and unresponsive audiences. One skill which the most successful comics perfected was timing—in the words they used and the order in which they used them, and their rhythm. But even more important was the way in which they stimulated audience participation. They would set up jokes so that the audience supplied the punchlines in their own minds, which gave them a feeling that they were part of the performance, and that they and the comedian were putting on the show together.

They made their audiences feel as if they were part of a conspiracy of amusement which nobody else could share, and this intimacy between performer and spectator won them enormous affection and success. You could call it "creative collaboration."

Max Miller, the "Cheekie Chappie" comedian of the 1950s, was especially adept at this. He would come on stage but repeatedly look towards the wings, where he told his audience that the manager of the theatre was watching to make sure that he didn't tell any off-colour jokes. Then he would lean forward to the audience and tell them some story like the one about the time when he was walking along a very narrow cliff path and saw a beautiful blonde coming towards him. The path was too narrow for them to pass each other, he said, so he didn't know whether to walk back the way he had come or toss himself off.

Or he would say, 'The search for the man who terrorises nudist camps with a bacon slicer goes on. Inspector Jones had a tip off this morning but, but hopes to be back on duty next week.'

When the audience laughed at this, he would blame them for having filthy minds, but they loved him for it.

Writers can build up the same rapport with their readership by using suggestive words—not only sexually suggestive, of course, but suggestive of horror, or anger, or appetites of any kind. These are words which will trigger a response that the writer knows lies dormant in their readers' minds. In one horror novel I wrote, for example, I described two young girls being "clubbed like seals." That was all I had to write for readers to picture it. One woman wrote to me and criticised me for writing such a bloody scenario, and it was only when I suggested that she go back and read it again and see that there was no blood mentioned that she understood that her reaction had all been in her own mind.

A carefully chosen image or reference can save authors the trouble of having to write a long-winded and graphic scenario. More importantly, though, it can recruit their readers into becoming accessories in the creation of their imaginary worlds and their imaginary characters—even though the readers themselves may not be aware of it. It gives readers a sense of involvement which heightens their feeling that the events in the story are real and it involves them much more in the destiny of the story's protagonists.

Timing is crucial, too. If you watch any of the recordings of Max Miller's performances, or those of other successful stand-up comedians, you can soon see that when they tell a joke they often pause at a critical moment to give their audience a few seconds to anticipate what the eventual outcome is going to be, and this heightens their involvement and their amusement. When they eventually come out with the punchline, they frequently come out with it in a rush, so that the audience is left stunned for a few seconds, and has to work out the twist for themselves. This adds to their sense of being co-conspirators in the story, and can often elicit tremendous laughs from a fairly unfunny joke.

I wrote a crime thriller called *Unspeakable* about a deaf social worker who helped the police by lip-reading the conversations of criminals in restaurants and other locations where it would have been difficult to plant a microphone. She was a very sympathetic and attractive character but right on the very last page a jilted lover sends a messenger around with a bouquet of yellow roses, and the messenger shoots her through a blizzard of petals. The end. The reaction I received from readers was extraordinary. Several said that they were left in tears. Almost all said that the ending was so terse and so unexpected that they sat with the book in their lap and their mouths open in shock.

If you take the trouble to study the routines of some of the most polished stand-up comedians you will learn a great deal about rhythm and delivery. You will also acquire a tremendous repertoire of jokes which you can tell whenever you're addressing an audience, from one-liners to long shaggy-dog stories. One of the toughest audiences I had to face was the inmates of Wołow maximum security prison in Poland—a hundred long-term prisoners with shaved heads and tattoos and eyes like two nail-heads. The first thing I said to them was, 'I can't stand people who take drugs.'

Their hostility was instant and almost palpable. But then I said, 'Like policemen and customs officers.' The prisoners laughed, and the atmosphere relaxed, and after that they became like enthusiastic readers.

When you write, forget that there's a page in front of you, or a PC screen. Imagine there's an audience who is longing for you to entertain them, and that they're more than willing to help you to do it.

As Max Miller would say, "Mary had a baby bear, to which she was so kind. And everywhere that Mary went, you could see her bear behind."

"Write as if you're not afraid of what people think."—**Chimamanda Ngozi Adichie**

Chapter 3

Establishing a Writing Foundation as a new author

The journey of a new author is exciting and daunting in equal measure. In the digital age, simply writing a book is not enough. Building a strong foundation is crucial for success. This foundation encompasses several key areas: personal branding, establishing an online presence, and engaging with writing communities.

Personal Branding: Personal branding is more than a buzzword—it's about carving out your unique space in the literary world. For an author, this means developing a distinct voice and style, both in your writing and how you present yourself publicly. Your brand should reflect who you are as a writer and what readers can expect from your work. It's this identity that will make you recognizable and relatable to your audience. This can take years, so start with something small, like a specific color palette or theme for your website and social media pages. If someone looks at all your platforms, they should recognize a common pattern, look, or feel. For some authors it's a style of clothing or even a hat.

Building a Website: A professional website is the cornerstone of an author's online presence. It's a platform you completely control, unlike social media or third-party sites. Your website should include information about you and your work, a blog or news section for updates, and links to purchase your books. It can also feature a sign-up option for newsletters, allowing you to build and maintain a direct relationship with your readers. Even if there isn't much to share yet, make sure you always have a website, especially when you start selling your first short stories. You want a link in that bio that'll take people somewhere you control. And it's never too early to start capturing emails for your mailing list.

Social Media Presence: Social media is a powerful tool for authors to connect with readers, promote their work, and build a community. Platforms like X, Instagram, and Facebook allow authors to share updates, engage in conversations, and participate in broader literary discussions. However, it's important to choose platforms that align with your brand and where your target audience is most active. Consistency in posting and engagement is key to growing a social media presence.

Joining Writing Forums and Communities: Participating in writing forums and communities is invaluable for new authors. These platforms offer a space to seek advice, receive feedback, and connect with peers and mentors. Communities like writing groups, both online and offline, provide support, inspiration, and learning opportunities. Engaging in these communities can also keep you informed about industry trends and opportunities, such as writing contests or publishing tips. I don't know what would've happened to me if it wasn't for the old Mywriterscircle.com forum.

Establishing a writing foundation as a new author involves a mix of creative and strategic efforts. Personal branding helps define your identity as a writer. A well-crafted website serves as your digital hub. An active social media presence allows you to connect with readers and promote your work. Finally, being part of writing communities offers support, learning, and growth opportunities. By focusing on these areas, new authors can build a solid foundation for a successful writing career.

Crafting an Effective Online Presence

In the digital age, a strong online presence is crucial for authors, especially in the horror genre. A well-crafted website and social media pages can significantly enhance a writer's visibility, engagement, and ultimately, success. Horror writers should aim to create a digital persona that reflects their unique brand while engaging their audience effectively.

A horror writer's website should be more than just a digital business card. It should be an immersive experience. Key elements include:

- Aesthetic and Theme: The website should reflect the horror genre's essence—it could be dark, mysterious, or even subtly unsettling. This thematic consistency helps in branding.

- About Section: This should provide a glimpse into the author's journey, influences, and style. It's an opportunity to connect on a personal level with readers, no matter where you currently are on your writing journey. People, especially readers, love an underdog story, so if you're a newbie with big dreams, don't shy away from that.

- Book Showcase: Highlight published works with cover images, synopses, and purchase links. Including reviews and testimonials can also add credibility. This includes short stories, guest blogs, podcast appearances, etc.

- Blog: Regularly updated blogs can offer insights into the author's thoughts on writing, horror themes, and industry trends. It's a platform for engaging content that goes beyond book promotion. Do not attempt this if you're already struggling to find time to write. And start out at a pace you can maintain, even if it's just once a month.

- Newsletter Sign-Up: Email newsletters are a direct line to readers, offering updates, exclusive content, or early access to new material. Social media platforms might change or disappear over time, but email marketing will always be there.

Social media is a dynamic tool for building a community and promoting content. Key strategies include:

- Consistent Branding: The horror theme should extend to social media. Use consistent profile pictures, banners, and posting styles.

- Engaging Content: Mix promotional posts with content that adds value—behind-the-scenes glimpses, horror trivia, writing tips, or interactive posts like polls and Q&As. If you know your target audience, you'll know what they like.

- Interaction: Respond to comments, engage with followers, and be part of the community. Authentic interaction can build loyal fanbases. That also means joining certain groups or pages without promoting your work over and over.

- Cross-Promotion: Use social media to direct traffic to the website, blog, or newsletter sign-up, creating a cohesive online ecosystem. Google will place your website higher in searches when you have more backlinks to your website.

Studying the websites and social media pages of a wide range of authors, not just in horror, can provide valuable insights. I'd recommend taking notes while analyzing at least 100 websites and 100 social media pages of diverse authors. This can reveal what resonates with readers:

Look for elements that consistently attract engagement—interactive features, multimedia content, personal anecdotes, and regular updates.

Notice what kinds of posts generate comments, shares, and likes. These often include storytelling, reader involvement, and relatable content.

While it's important to observe what's effective for others, it's crucial to adapt these strategies to fit your unique brand. There is only one you, so if you can take what works for others and mesh it with who you are (your life and world view, personality, sense of humor, etc.), that's where you create a brand that stands out. That's where you will eventually find your unique voice.

Chapter 4

Mastering the Art of a Book Launch
Part 1 (part 2 coming in book 2)

A book launch is a pivotal moment for any author, be it in the realm of traditional or self-publishing. While the paths may differ, the core essentials of a successful book launch remain largely the same. Let's look at the critical steps an author should take to ensure a successful launch.

Understanding Your Book and Audience: Firstly, it's essential to have a deep understanding of your book. This involves fine-tuning the book description and researching relevant keywords and categories. I'd recommend using for that. I use it every single day. So whether you're self-publishing or working with a publisher, providing input on these aspects can significantly impact your book's visibility. Keywords and categories not only aid in discoverability on platforms like Amazon but also help in crafting a compelling book description that resonates with your target audience. Remember, you'll appear much higher on Amazon searches if your keywords are present in your description. For non-fiction books, make sure your best keywords are in the subtitle (like the book you're holding right now; some non-fiction subtitles can be incredibly long). For fiction, you can slip in something like Suspense Thriller or Horror Novella. But keep the subtitle short.

Building Relationships and Buzz: Developing industry relationships is vital. For instance, reaching out for blurb requests to authors in your genre can add credibility to your book. Beta-readers are invaluable in providing early feedback, and sending advance copies to reviewers who have appreciated your past work can lead to early positive reviews, creating pre-launch buzz.

Social media plays a crucial role in modern book marketing. Creating eye-catching artwork for your social media posts can attract attention and engage potential readers. It's important to start building excitement about your upcoming launch well in advance. Utilize platforms like X, Instagram, and Facebook to share teasers, countdowns, and behind-the-scenes glimpses of your launch preparation. If you have the skills or programs like , you can even create short videos for YouTube, Instagram, and TikTok.

Leveraging Different Platforms: Securing guest spots on podcasts and writing guest posts for blogs can expand your reach. These platforms offer an opportunity to connect with new audiences, share insights about your book, and talk about your writing journey.

Prepping your newsletter is another crucial step. Newsletters allow for direct communication with your readers and can be used to announce your book launch, share exclusive content, or provide sneak peeks. It's vital that you tell a story here. Don't just promote your book. Dive deep into personal aspects about why you chose this story. Which themes resonate with you and your life. Share the journey, especially the hard parts.

Innovative Marketing Strategies: A creative marketing strategy involves giving something of value to your audience. Writing a short story set in the same universe as your book and offering it for free is an excellent way to entice new readers. This approach can be particularly effective in building your mailing list. Pairing this with targeted Facebook ads showcasing the short story can broaden your reach and help accumulate a list of interested readers ahead of your launch. They see the genre-appropriate artwork and enticing title, click on the ad, go to a funnel page (there are cheaper options, but I'm a big fan of), read more about the story and your upcoming release, and then, hopefully, type in their email so that they can receive the free story. And before running this ad and giveaway, you can also share this short story with your existing mailing list to build up the excitement for the launch.

Preparing for a book launch is a multifaceted effort that involves understanding your product and audience, building and nurturing industry relationships, creating engaging promotional content, leveraging various platforms for exposure, and employing innovative marketing strategies. Regardless of the publishing route, these foundational steps are crucial for a successful book launch. By carefully planning and executing these strategies, authors can maximize their reach and set the stage for a successful introduction of their work to the world. We'll discuss the actual book launch in *Shadows & Ink Vol.2.*

Launches That Sustain a Long-Term Writing Career

Launching a book is a significant milestone in any author's journey, yet it's essential to remember that a successful writing career extends far beyond a single publication. It's about continual growth, building connections, and consistently planning for the future. Here, we'll explore how to not only launch your book effectively but also lay the foundation for long-term success in the literary world.

Thinking Beyond the Current Launch: While your immediate focus might be on your current book launch, it's crucial to also think ahead to your next project. Continuously producing new work keeps your audience engaged and maintains momentum in your career. Planning, or even beginning, your next book during your current launch keeps readers excited about your upcoming work. Consider taking a short break between projects, perhaps to write a short story or two, allowing you to recharge and return to your next big story with renewed energy.

Building and Nurturing Industry Contacts: Networking is a cornerstone of the publishing industry. Actively building your contact list with industry professionals—including publishers, agents, reviewers, bloggers, other authors, and marketing experts—can lead to new opportunities and collaborations. Engage in mutual support, such as assisting with their book launches, supporting their initiatives, or sharing their successes. This not only strengthens your network but also builds lasting professional relationships and friendships.

Expanding Your Mailing List: Your mailing list is a vital tool, offering a direct connection to your most dedicated readers. Work continuously on expanding this list by offering enticing incentives, such as exclusive content or sneak peeks of upcoming works. Regular engagement with your subscribers through updates, insights, and personal anecdotes keeps your readership involved and invested in your journey. Remember, if you sell one book to a reader, the relationship might very well end there. With your next launch, you need to find that reader again. By building your mailing list, you're improving your reach on a day-to-day basis.

Ensuring Longevity in Your Career: Building a successful writing career is a long-term endeavor, filled with both triumphs and challenges. Every experience, whether a successful launch or a setback, offers valuable lessons. Embrace feedback, experiment with different strategies, and continuously refine your craft. As a publisher who has launched almost 200 books over a decade, I've learned the importance of trying new things and learning from each experience. This approach keeps you adaptable and fearless in your career.

Social Media Do's and Don'ts: Social media is a double-edged sword. It's essential for building a presence and connecting with readers, but it must be used wisely.

- Do: Be authentic and engage genuinely with your audience. Share updates, insights, and content that add value. Use social media to build a community around your work.

- Don't: Over-promote or spam your followers with constant sales pitches. Avoid getting involved in controversies or negative interactions that could harm your professional reputation. That means staying away from politics and religion. We all know that no matter what you say, you can't win. You are not there to change people's minds about the world. Which, by the way, we do by example. Or by words on the page, not words on a tweet or post.

Remember, the launch of your current book is just one step in a much larger journey. Focus on your long-term goals, and view each event as a building block toward a greater objective. Your writing career should aim to create a legacy of stories that not only resonate with readers today but also stand the test of time.

Incorporating these strategies will not only enhance your current book launch but also pave the way for a sustainable, rewarding writing career. Each step you take is an opportunity to strengthen your presence in the literary world, forge meaningful connections, and hone your storytelling skills. A successful writing career is about more than just one book. It's about crafting a legacy of impactful stories.

> *"Amateurs sit and wait for inspiration, the rest of us just get up and go to work."*—**Stephen King**

Chapter 5

Time Management

Time management in the life of a writer is more than just a skill—it's an art. It's about understanding and accepting the natural rhythm of good days and bad days, especially when it comes to how many words we can craft. For writers, staying positive amidst this fluctuating productivity is essential.

Every writer experiences days when the words flow effortlessly, and others when it feels like pulling teeth to write even a single sentence. It's important to recognize that this is a normal part of the creative process. On days when the word count is low, it's crucial to ward off negative thoughts. These moments of struggle are not a reflection of your abilities or potential as a writer.

The key to managing these fluctuations is to take each day as it comes. Celebrate the successful days when the words pour out, but also embrace the slower days as necessary pauses in your creative journey. These pauses can be times of subconscious brewing, where ideas simmer and develop in the background.

The most important thing is to keep moving forward, recognizing that some days you'll make giant strides and others, smaller steps. The cumulative effect of consistent writing, regardless of the daily word count, is what leads to finished pieces.

Discovering and harnessing what motivates you can be a game-changer in managing your time and productivity. Motivators can vary widely among writers and can even change from week to week. For some, it could be the quiet of early morning hours, for others, the bustling energy of a café.

Personally, I find great motivation in listening to motivational speakers. A quick 5-minute video on YouTube can sometimes be all it takes to reignite me. These external sources of inspiration can act as catalysts, helping to jumpstart the writing process on days when internal motivation might be lacking.

Embracing that what motivates you might change over time is part of the journey. Be open to exploring new sources of inspiration and new routines. Flexibility in your approach to writing and time management can lead to discovering more effective strategies that align with your evolving needs and circumstances. And yes, that includes aging.

Writing, while a fulfilling pursuit, often has to share space with our day jobs, family responsibilities, and personal life. Balancing these can feel like trying to keep plates spinning on sticks. But fear not! With some smart strategies, you can keep those plates spinning smoothly. Let's dive into some practical advice for managing your time effectively.

Embrace the Power of Routine: For authors, managing time effectively is not just a skill, it's an art. It involves identifying your most productive hours and committing to a consistent routine. The first step is to figure out whether you're a night owl, who finds their creative spark in the quiet hours of the night, or an early bird, whose best ideas flow in the calm of the early morning. Once you've pinpointed these 'golden hours,' dedicate them to your writing. This could mean setting your alarm an hour earlier or carving out time after dinner when the world is winding down. For me personally, most of this book is being written between the hours of 5AM and 8AM, since my nights are normally filled with Zoom meetings.

Consistency in your writing schedule is crucial. Strive to write at the same time each day. By doing so, you're training your brain to enter 'writing mode' at these regular intervals. This regularity not only helps in establishing a disciplined approach but also enhances your mental preparedness and focus during these times. It's also a great way to let the people in your life know when you're not available.

Remember, routine isn't about restricting your creativity; it's about creating a framework within which your creativity can flourish. It's about making the most of the time you have, whether it's a full day or just an hour, to advance your writing goals. Effective time management as an author means balancing discipline with flexibility, ensuring that your writing life coexists harmoniously with your other responsibilities and pleasures.

> *"Often writers will stop the day's work at the end of a scene or chapter. I try my best not to do that. If I stop in the middle of a chapter, a scene, or even at times a sentence, the next day I will find myself right back in the middle of action or adventure. This makes it all the easier to get going again, instead of staring at the page wondering what I should write next."*—**Elizabeth Massie**

Set Realistic Goals: Achieving success as an author often comes down to setting and meeting realistic goals. It's about understanding the power of small, manageable steps and how they can lead to significant results over time.

Instead of setting your sights on daunting, overarching goals, try breaking them down into smaller, more achievable tasks. This could mean setting a daily word count target or dedicating a fixed amount of time to write each day. For instance, consistently writing 500 words each day might seem modest, but it can lead to a substantial novel-length manuscript in a year. By breaking down your goals, you make the task of writing a book seem less overwhelming and more attainable.

Every small goal you achieve brings you one step closer to completing your project. It's important to acknowledge and celebrate these milestones. Did you hit your daily word count? Finish a tricky chapter? Work through a difficult plot point? Celebrate these achievements! This not only provides a sense of accomplishment but also keeps your motivation high. Remember, every word written is progress, and every small victory is a building block in your journey as an author.

It's all a balance of ambition and practicality, ensuring that you make steady progress without burning out. By setting and celebrating achievable goals, you can maintain a sustainable and rewarding writing practice.

Prioritize and Plan: For authors juggling writing with other life commitments, mastering the art of prioritization and planning is essential.

I highly recommend a weekly to-do list. Begin each week by laying out a clear plan. What are your writing objectives for the week? Do you have any personal or professional commitments that need to be factored in? By putting everything down on a list, whether on paper or digitally, you gain a bird's-eye view of your week. This clarity allows you to allocate your time more effectively, balancing writing goals with other responsibilities. It helps in setting realistic expectations for what you can accomplish and prevents overcommitting yourself.

My to-do-list is a monthly calendar on Excel, with a clear list for every day, a few open spots for any issues or opportunities that arise, along with an overarching goal for that week. Normally something like learning or practicing a skill.

It's crucial to also recognize that you can't do everything. Learning to say no is an invaluable skill. When you're invited to events or asked to take on additional tasks that don't align with your key priorities, it's okay to decline. Remember, every time you say 'yes' to something, you're effectively saying 'no' to something else—often, your writing. Prioritizing your writing doesn't mean neglecting other aspects of your life, but it does require making conscious choices about how you spend your time.

As you can see, effective time management for authors revolves around thoughtful planning and the ability to set boundaries. By clearly defining your weekly goals and being selective about your commitments, you can ensure that your writing remains a top priority, paving the way for a more productive and fulfilling writing journey.

Use Technology Wisely: In today's digital age, authors have the advantage of technology to streamline their writing and time management processes.

- Exploring Writing Applications: There are numerous writing apps available that can significantly enhance your writing efficiency. Tools like Scrivener or Google Docs are excellent for organizing your work. Scrivener, for instance, offers a robust platform for managing large writing projects, allowing you to organize notes, research, and drafts all in one place. Google Docs provides the flexibility of cloud-based access, enabling you to write from anywhere. These apps not only save time but also keep your thoughts and work structured, making the writing process smoother and more manageable.

- Time Management Tools for Writers: To keep a tab on your various tasks and deadlines, consider using time management tools like Trello or Asana. These tools allow you to create boards or lists for different projects or aspects of your writing, such as research, drafting, editing, and marketing. You can set deadlines, prioritize tasks, and track your progress. This kind of organization helps maintain a clear focus on your goals and ensures that you are making consistent progress without feeling overwhelmed. I personally just use an Excel spreadsheet laid out like a calendar, with just enough space on each day that I don't get overwhelmed, and still have enough time for my family.

By wisely incorporating technology into your writing practice, you can enhance your productivity and keep better track of your writing goals and deadlines. These digital tools can help organize your writing process, manage your time effectively, and ultimately contribute to a more structured and stress-free writing experience.

Find a Balance: For authors, finding the right balance between writing and personal life is crucial for both productivity and well-being.

- Valuing Personal Time: Writing is a demanding task, both mentally and emotionally. It's essential to remember that taking time off to recharge is not just beneficial, it's necessary. Ensure you set aside time regularly for relaxation and activities that bring you joy, whether it's pursuing a hobby, reading, or simply unwinding. Equally important is spending quality time with family and friends. These moments away from writing are not just breaks. They are opportunities to replenish your creative energy and maintain a healthy work-life balance.

- Embracing Flexibility: No matter how well you plan, there will be days when things don't go as expected. Interruptions, unplanned events, or simply days when the words don't flow as easily are all part of the writing life. On such days, it's important to stay flexible. Adjust your schedule and goals accordingly. Flexibility in managing your writing time helps reduce stress and prevents burnout. It's about understanding that productivity isn't always linear and that taking a step back can sometimes be as valuable as pushing forward.

Stay Healthy: Maintaining good health is vital for authors, as it directly impacts creativity and productivity.

- Taking Care of Physical Health: Regular physical exercise, a balanced diet, and sufficient sleep are fundamental for a writer. A healthy body supports a healthy mind, essential for creativity. Exercise, even something as simple as a daily walk or stretching routine, can greatly enhance mental clarity and energy levels. A nutritious diet keeps the body fueled, and getting enough rest ensures that you are mentally and physically ready for the demands of writing. Remember, taking care of your physical health is not a luxury; it's a necessity for maintaining the stamina and focus required for writing.

- Importance of Mental Breaks: Writing is an intensive mental activity, and continuous writing without breaks can lead to burnout. Incorporate short, regular breaks into your writing sessions. Use this time to take a quick walk, enjoy a cup of tea, or simply step outside for fresh air. These brief pauses are not just for relaxation; they provide an opportunity for your mind to rest and reset, often leading to new insights and ideas when you return to your writing.

Staying healthy is crucial for writers. By taking care of your physical and mental well-being, you ensure that you have the energy, clarity, and endurance needed to pursue your writing goals effectively. Regular exercise, a balanced diet, adequate sleep, and taking mental breaks are all key components of a healthy writing lifestyle.

Seek Support: We'll cover more of this important aspect in the next chapter, but for now, understand that every writer needs a solid support system, since the journey can often be challenging and solitary.

- Connecting with Writing Communities: Joining writing groups or communities, whether online or in-person, can be incredibly beneficial. These groups provide a sense of camaraderie and accountability, which is often crucial for staying motivated and productive. Being part of a community allows you to share experiences, challenges, and successes with others who understand the unique nature of the writing process. Additionally, such groups can be a great source of feedback, encouragement, and inspiration.

- Engaging Family and Friends: Don't underestimate the importance of support from your family and friends. Share your writing aspirations and goals with them. Their encouragement and understanding can be a huge morale booster, especially during times when writing feels particularly challenging. Their support can manifest in various ways, from providing you with uninterrupted time to write, to offering a listening ear when you need to talk through a tricky plot point or character development.

Whether it's finding kinship in writing groups or leaning on the encouragement of family and friends, having a network of support can greatly enhance your writing experience and contribute to your success as an author.

Reflect and Adjust: Make it a habit to pause at the end of each week and conduct a self-review. Reflect on your accomplishments and challenges. What writing strategies were effective? Where did you face obstacles? This reflection helps in identifying areas for improvement. Use these insights to fine-tune your approach, making necessary adjustments to your writing schedule and techniques for the upcoming week. This cycle of reflection and adjustment is key to evolving and enhancing your writing process. What I found works for me, and is extremely vital, is to completely step away from everything once a week, even if just for 20 minutes. I step back and try to look at everything I'm doing as one big thing. I allow myself to feel pride but also look at where I can grow. I wish I could tell you how many of my great ideas and projects were born out of this reflection time. The book you're holding right now, for instance.

Balancing writing with other life commitments is a skill that develops over time. By setting realistic goals, establishing a routine, and using the right tools, you can make writing a natural part of your life. Remember, the key is not to find more time, but to make the most of the time you have. Happy writing!

"*It's a rare writer who is at a place in her craft and career where she can write in complete isolation, finish a story, send it off to an editor, and have that work see print. The vast majority of us need feedback on our work before it's ready for an editor's eyes.*"—**Lucy A. Snyder, author of *Sister, Maiden, Monster***

Chapter 6

Seeking Help and Building a Support System for Writers

Gone are the days when writers were expected to toil in isolation, with only their thoughts for company. In the modern era of writing, seeking help and building a supportive community have become integral parts of the creative process. This essay delves into the importance of asking for help, joining groups or mentoring programs, attending workshops, and creating a support system that not only offers guidance but also holds you accountable.

Breaking the Myth of the Lone Writer: The romanticized image of the solitary writer is fading, making way for a more collaborative and interactive approach to writing. Today, seeking help is not a sign of weakness but a recognition of the multifaceted nature of writing. By reaching out, writers can gain new perspectives, enhance their skills, and navigate the complex world of publishing more effectively.

Joining Groups and Mentoring Programs: Joining a writing group or a mentoring program can be a transformative experience. These platforms provide opportunities to connect with fellow writers, share experiences, and learn from each other. Mentoring programs, in particular, offer personalized guidance, helping writers to hone their craft under the tutelage of experienced authors. These interactions can lead to lasting relationships, providing a network of support throughout one's writing career.

The Value of Workshops: Workshops are another invaluable resource for writers. They offer a structured environment where one can learn new techniques, receive feedback, and engage in critical discussions. Workshops also provide a space to experiment and take creative risks in a supportive setting. They can be especially beneficial for writers looking to break out of creative ruts or those seeking to expand their stylistic boundaries.

Building a Support System: Creating a support system is crucial for sustained productivity and growth. This system can include writing groups, online forums, beta readers, and mentors. Each component plays a unique role:

- Writing Groups: Offer camaraderie and a sense of community. They are spaces for sharing work, receiving feedback, and mutual encouragement.

- Online Forums: Provide a broader platform to connect with writers worldwide, exchange ideas, and stay updated on industry trends.

- Beta Readers: Are essential for gaining unbiased feedback on your work. They can point out areas that need improvement before the manuscript reaches the public.

- Mentors: Mentoring is an invaluable asset for budding writers, offering a unique combination of personal support, professional insight, and practical guidance. Unlike general writing advice, a mentor provides personalized feedback tailored to an individual's specific needs and challenges. This might include refining narrative voice, improving plot structure, or developing characters, with the mentor's experienced eye identifying and helping to rectify issues that might otherwise be overlooked.

Moreover, the publishing world can be daunting for new authors. A mentor not only brings writing expertise but also valuable industry knowledge. They can guide budding writers through the intricacies of the publishing process, from understanding market dynamics to navigating submissions and even the business aspects of writing. This industry insight is crucial for avoiding common pitfalls and is often hard to gain through research alone.

Creative blocks and periods of doubt are common in a writer's journey. Here, a mentor acts as a source of motivation and a sounding board, providing encouragement and strategies to overcome these hurdles based on their own experiences. The accountability provided by regular check-ins with a mentor ensures consistent progress, helping to instill discipline and a professional approach to writing.

Mentoring is a catalyst for growth and success in writing. It accelerates development, helps navigate the complex writing and publishing landscape, and offers the support and accountability necessary for aspiring writers to succeed. For those serious about a career in writing, seeking a mentor can be a pivotal step toward realizing their potential and achieving their goals.

Accountability and Growth: A crucial aspect of a support system is accountability. Regular check-ins with a writing group or a mentor can keep you on track, helping you meet your goals and deadlines. This accountability ensures that you not only maintain a steady output but also continuously improve your craft.

The act of asking for help and building a support system is fundamental to a writer's journey. It fosters a sense of community, encourages continuous learning, and keeps writers accountable. By embracing the resources available, writers can enrich their craft, broaden their perspectives, and navigate their careers with greater confidence and support. Whether it's through joining groups, attending workshops, or connecting with mentors, these steps are essential in building a fulfilling and sustainable writing career.

Mastermind groups

A mastermind group is a collaborative assembly where individuals pay to join and benefit from the collective wisdom and experience of the group. Each member brings their unique skills and perspectives, contributing to the group's overall knowledge and growth. A designated facilitator or 'mastermind' leads the group, ensuring structured discussions and goal-oriented sessions. This set-up allows members to learn from each other, gain insights, and receive support in achieving their personal or professional objectives, fostering an environment of mutual growth and accountability.

If you're serious about your writing career and you are either already published (self or traditional) or have a book out soon, I highly recommend joining the . It's only $150 for a full year, and there's no other place where you can connect with so many industry professionals twice a month. All online. Other bonuses include joint projects and the use of a mailing list we're all building together. If you're already part of our Heartbeat community, it's a simple upgrade. Contact me there if you get stuck.

Exploring the Shadows & Ink Heartbeat Community

In the dynamic and often solitary world of horror writing, the importance of a supportive community cannot be overstated. The Shadows & Ink Heartbeat community emerges as a beacon, offering a unique and nurturing environment tailored specifically for those who delve into the realm of horror literature. It's a place where the macabre, the eerie, and the spine-chilling are not just understood but celebrated.

Shadows & Ink Heartbeat is more than a mere gathering of writers. It's a sanctuary for creators of terror and suspense. This community provides a free and inclusive setting, welcoming authors at all stages of their journey. Here, horror writers can engage in meaningful conversations about their craft, share their work for feedback, and imbibe fresh perspectives on the genre. The foundation of the community is built on collaboration, learning, and mutual support, creating a vibrant space for creative growth.

For those who seek deeper engagement, offers several paid tiers. The $10-a-month tier is recommended to authors with upcoming book release (or who already have book for sale). The $150-a-year tier is of course for the Master-mind group. All the tiers, including the free tier, include workshops and courses. This tiered approach caters to a range of needs, from authors just starting to those setting up their book launches.

An essential component of this community is the Heartbeat app, which acts as a digital companion for horror authors. This app is a hub for community interactions, offering easy access to forums, discussions, and a wealth of resources. It's a practical tool for managing writing schedules, setting goals, and tracking progress. The app enriches the experience with its extensive library of horror-specific resources, including insightful articles, writing prompts, and genre-focused tips.

In essence, Shadows & Ink Heartbeat is not just about forming connections. It's about fostering growth and success in the exhilarating field of horror writing, and keeping our fellow authors motivated and on track. It's a space where horror authors can find their tribe, refine their craft, and thrive in a community that understands the unique challenges and joys of writing horror. For anyone passionate about horror literature, is the ideal convergence of community, learning, and technological support, all aimed at nurturing the creative spirit of horror writers. This is where I hang out while working. I also share everything new I learn on Heartbeat, which means you can keep writing and we'll all help each other stay up to date with the latest technology, trends, resources, free courses, etc. It's time we all stand together like never before.

Chapter 7

Don't Give Up
by Tom Deady

I've known I wanted to be a writer since I was ten years old. I was obsessed with my brother's collection of Hardy Boys books and devoured them one after another. At some point I tried writing my own story about...you guessed it: two brothers who solve mysteries. But it fizzled.

When I was in high school, I discovered Stephen King, tearing through *Salem's Lot* in record time. When my English teacher gave us a creative writing assignment, I wrote a short story about...vampires. She loved the story and wrote next to my grade, "Let's put it in Boojum Rock!" That was our high school magazine. I declined, too much the introvert to want others to read my work.

I did some writing in college, even going so far as submitting a couple of stories. When they were rejected, I became discouraged. Years later, I took a mail-order writing course through Writer's Digest magazine (yes, mail-order, this was 1995!). That was when I officially began writing the novel that would become *Haven*, using the old blue-screen WordPerfect program on my work computer during lunch breaks.

Work, night school, raising two daughters, and more work...turned into a fifteen-year period of fits and starts working on the novel. Finally, it was completed in 2012!

Haven was picked up by Cemetery Dance and sold out the limited-edition hardcover. It went on to win the Bram Stoker Award for Superior Achievement in a First Novel.

I have since published several novels, novellas, short stories, and non-fiction articles, and have even shared a table of contents with Stephen King!

Follow your dreams, no matter how long it takes.

> *"A reader lives a thousand lives before he dies. The man who never reads lives only one."*—**George R.R. Martin**

Chapter 8

Handling sensitive topics, violence, and ensuring responsible story-telling.

In the world of storytelling, particularly in genres like horror or dark fiction, authors often tread on sensitive ground. Handling topics like violence, trauma, or controversial themes requires a delicate balance. It's not just about what you say, but how you say it. Let's explore how to approach these sensitive topics responsibly and ethically.

1. Understanding the Impact of Your Words
   - Power of Influence: Recognize that as a writer, your words have power. They can influence perceptions, evoke strong emotions, and even shape attitudes.

   - Empathy and Respect: Approach sensitive topics with empathy and respect. Consider the impact your story may have on readers, especially those who have experienced similar situations.

2. Research Thoroughly
   - Get the Facts Right: When dealing with topics outside your personal experience, research is key. Misrepresentation can not only break the immersion of your story but also offend or harm.

- Consult Experts: If possible, consult with experts or individuals who have lived experiences relevant to your story. This can add authenticity and sensitivity to your portrayal.

3. Handling Violence, Trauma, and Gore
- Show Consequences: When depicting violence or trauma, show the consequences. This adds depth to your story and avoids glorifying or trivializing the experience.

- Sensitive Portrayal: Be mindful of how you describe these events. Graphic details may not always be necessary and can be distressing for some readers.

- Purposeful Inclusion: Violence or sensitive content should serve a purpose in your story. Gratuitous or sensationalized depictions can be seen as exploitative. Unless this is the target market you're writing for. Know your audience.

- Impact vs. Shock Value: Aim for impact, not shock. Shock fades, but impact stays with the reader, prompting thought and discussion.

4. Cultural Sensitivity
- Avoid Stereotypes: Steer clear of stereotypes, especially when writing about cultures or experiences different from your own. Stereotypes are not only lazy writing but can perpetuate harmful myths.

- Cultural Respect: Show respect for the cultures and experiences you are portraying. This means avoiding cultural appropriation and ensuring accurate representation.

5. Trigger Warnings

- Consider Warnings: Been a slightly confrontational topic lately. Comes down to this. As an editor/publisher, I go with what the editor or authors want. I give them that option. As an author, you need to make that decision based on what your readers want. And if you don't know what they want, you have no job writing a story for them. At least not yet. For particularly intense or potentially triggering content, consider including a trigger warning. This respects the reader's choice to engage with the material. Not everyone is currently a fan of using trigger warnings in horror fiction, but decide for yourself and respect the opinions of others.

6. Open to Feedback

- Seek Diverse Perspectives: Before publishing, get feedback from a diverse range of readers. They may catch insensitivities you missed.

- Be Open to Criticism: If criticized for your portrayal, listen and learn. It's an opportunity to grow as a writer and a person. Just be sure to do that before the actual publication.

7. Ethical Storytelling

- Moral Responsibility: Remember, you have a moral responsibility as a storyteller. Your stories can open minds, but they can also wound. Strive to tell stories that are not only engaging but also respectful and considerate.

Navigating sensitive topics in storytelling is a complex task that requires thoughtfulness, research, and empathy. By approaching these topics with care and responsibility, you can craft stories that are not only compelling but also respectful and enlightening. As a writer, your ultimate goal should be to tell a story that resonates with truth and humanity, regardless of the darkness of its themes.

Chapter 9

One Step Back, Two Steps Forward
by Jessica Landry

We celebrate our wins (and for good reason—be loud, be proud!), but with that comes the cost of our failures. Rejection is not an easy thing for anyone, at any time, anywhere. It's not something we want to bring attention to or remember for longer than we have to.

But rejection, as difficult, annoying, frustrating, heartbreaking, soul-crushing as it is, should be celebrated.

Why?

Because you took that leap, that bound, that step forward. You sent something born in your mind, something you raised and tended to and shaped, out into the world. You let others in to your most vulnerable self. And while the result may not have been what you hoped, dreamed, knew it would be, that isn't something to be ashamed of.

And while there are still many more rejections to come (because there always are, for everyone, at any time, anywhere), don't think of them as failures, as reasons to quit, as excuses.

Celebrate them like you celebrate your victories, because they're something to be proud of.

Chapter 10

Healthy Writing Habits

Mental health is a crucial aspect for all individuals, but it holds a unique significance for authors, particularly those who delve into the realms of horror. Horror authors often navigate through the darkest corridors of human experience, exploring themes like death, loss, violence, abuse, and past trauma. This journey, while artistically fulfilling, can also be a treacherous path for mental well-being.

The Emotional Toll of Writing Horror: Writing horror is an artistic endeavor that requires one to delve deeply into the realms of fear, anxiety, and the darker aspects of human nature. For authors who dare to traverse this genre, the journey is not merely about crafting stories. It involves a profound immersion in some of the most disturbing and discomforting themes. This exploration, while central to the creation of impactful horror narratives, exposes authors to a myriad of intense emotions that can often have a lasting impact.

Famed horror writers like Edgar Allan Poe often explored themes of death, madness, and the macabre. Poe's own life was marked by tragedy and loss, elements that deeply influenced his writing. The constant engagement with such dark themes could arguably have blurred the lines between his fiction and reality, contributing to the melancholic and often disturbed state that defined much of his life.

For horror writers, the repeated journey into stories filled with fear, death, and violence can have psychological consequences. They may experience a heightened sense of existential dread, a persistent awareness of life's darker realities that can be both emotionally taxing and profoundly isolating. Alternatively, some authors might find themselves becoming desensitized to emotional distress, as their constant exposure to horror themes normalizes what many would find deeply unsettling.

Moreover, the process of creating believable horror stories often requires writers to empathize with both the victim and the perpetrator, to understand their fears, motivations, and pain. This deep empathetic dive can be psychologically demanding, as it necessitates dwelling in a mental space where extreme human emotions and experiences are not just imagined, but vividly brought to life. As a result, the emotional toll of writing horror is a unique and complex challenge, one that intertwines with the very essence of what makes these stories resonate with their audience.

The Risk of Alcohol and Substance Abuse: The history of literature is riddled with tales of authors who struggled with alcohol and substance abuse. Notable examples include Ernest Hemingway, F. Scott Fitzgerald, and once again Edgar Allan Poe, who are as famous for their literary genius as they are for their tragic battles with addiction. The reasons behind such dependencies are complex, often rooted in a mix of personal, psychological, and societal factors. For some, alcohol or drugs may seem like a refuge from the emotional intensity of their writing or a means to stimulate creativity. However, this temporary solace can quickly spiral into dependency, exacerbating mental health issues and, in some cases, leading to tragic outcomes.

As horror authors who constantly delve into dark themes, we often face unique challenges regarding mental health. Recognizing and addressing these challenges is crucial for sustaining a healthy and productive writing career, before we start reaching out to vices.

Acknowledging and Addressing Mental Health: The first step is acknowledging the potential impact that constantly engaging with horror themes can have on one's mental health. This recognition is vital as it allows authors to understand their feelings and take proactive steps toward self-care. It's essential to monitor one's emotional state and be aware of any signs of distress or unease that may arise from the writing process. I tend to watch a lot more comedies than horror when it comes to movies and series, just to balance out my life a bit and add more laughter.

Professional Support: Seeking therapy or counseling can be a game-changer for horror authors. Mental health professionals are equipped to provide strategies and support for coping with the emotional toll of writing horror. They can also assist in addressing any underlying issues that might be exacerbated by the genre's dark themes.

Balancing Writing with Positive Activities: Counterbalancing the intensity of writing horror with uplifting and relaxing activities is crucial. Engaging in physical exercise, meditation, pursuing hobbies, or spending quality time with loved ones can provide much-needed mental respite. These activities not only offer a break from the writing process but also help in maintaining a well-rounded and healthy lifestyle.

Creating a Supportive Community (told you this was important): Building connections with fellow horror authors can be incredibly beneficial. A community of peers who understand the specific challenges of the genre can provide solidarity, comfort, and practical coping strategies. Sharing experiences and tips with one another can lead to new insights and mutual support.

Setting Boundaries: It is imperative for horror authors to set clear boundaries between their work and personal life. Knowing when to step back from writing and taking time to decompress is essential in preventing burnout. These boundaries ensure that writing horror doesn't consume one's life and helps maintain a healthy perspective.

Mindfulness and Reflection: Practicing mindfulness and reflection can help authors process the emotions and thoughts that arise during their writing. Techniques like journaling or meditation can offer a space for introspection and emotional release.

Embracing Creativity in a Positive Light: While horror writing delves into dark themes, it's also a form of creative expression. Embracing the positive aspects of crafting stories and the joy of creativity can provide a balanced perspective.

For horror authors, navigating the complexities of mental health is as important as honing their craft. The very act of exploring the depths of fear and trauma can take a toll, making self-care and mental health awareness paramount. By acknowledging the challenges and adopting healthy coping strategies, authors can not only safeguard their well-being but also enhance their ability to tell stories that are both profoundly disturbing and deeply human.

Healthy Writing Habits

Writing, often perceived as a sedentary and solitary activity, can take a toll on both physical and of course mental health. To maintain a sustainable writing practice, it's crucial to adopt healthy habits. Let's dive into some key areas: ergonomics, regular breaks, eye care, and exercises specifically beneficial for writers.

Ergonomics

- Investing in a Good Desk and Chair: The foundation of a healthy workspace is a comfortable, ergonomically designed chair, coupled with a desk of the correct height. Ensure that your feet can rest flat on the floor, with your knees at a 90-degree angle. Your desk should allow your arms to be positioned comfortably, with your elbows at a right angle while typing. This setup helps in maintaining good posture and reducing the risk of back and shoulder strain. If you have strong core muscles, consider sitting on a yoga ball.

- Optimal Monitor Positioning: The position of your monitor is key to avoiding neck and eye strain. The top of the screen should be at or slightly below eye level, positioned about an arm's length away. If you're using a laptop, consider using a laptop stand or an external keyboard and mouse to achieve the correct height and angle. This adjustment ensures that you're not hunching over or straining your neck while working.

- Choosing the Right Keyboard and Mouse: Select a keyboard and mouse that feel comfortable and natural in your hands. They should allow for a relaxed hand position without causing strain. Consider using wrist rests for additional support, as they can help in maintaining a neutral wrist position, preventing issues like carpal tunnel syndrome. Using a laptop without an external mouse can be detrimental to your wrists in the long run.

Regular Breaks

- The Pomodoro Technique: This time management method involves 25 minutes of focused writing followed by a 5-minute break. It's an effective way to enhance concentration and productivity while avoiding burnout. These short bursts of focused work, punctuated by brief breaks, allow you to maintain a steady pace without feeling overwhelmed. The technique also helps in tracking your progress and keeping you motivated through a sense of accomplishment.

- Stretching and Movement: During your breaks, it's important to physically move and stretch. Simple exercises like stretching your arms, legs, neck, and back, or taking a short walk around the room or outside, can do wonders. These activities increase blood circulation, reduce muscle tension, and can help prevent the stiffness and discomfort associated with prolonged sitting. Even a brief change of scenery and a bit of movement can re-energize you for the next writing session.

- Taking Mental Breaks: Breaks should also be about mental relaxation. Step away from writing and allow your mind to rest. This could mean doing something completely unrelated to writing, like a quick meditation, listening to a song, or simply enjoying a quiet moment. These mental breaks are crucial for maintaining creativity and perspective. They allow you to return to your work with a refreshed mind, often leading to clearer thinking and new ideas.

Eye Care

- The 20-20-20 Rule: To combat eye strain, try the 20-20-20 rule: every 20 minutes, shift your gaze to focus on an object at least 20 feet away for 20 seconds. This simple practice helps in relaxing your eye muscles, reducing the risk of fatigue, and keeping your eyes comfortable. It's an easy-to-remember routine that can make a significant difference in preventing the discomfort that comes from prolonged screen time.

- Adjusting Screen Brightness: To further protect your eyes, it's important to ensure that your screen brightness is not too harsh compared to your surrounding environment. A screen that's too bright or too dim can cause additional strain to your eyes. Adjusting the brightness to a comfortable level that blends well with the lighting in your room can help in reducing glare and strain.

- Regular Eye Exams: Regular check-ups with an eye care professional are essential, especially if you experience symptoms like frequent headaches, blurred vision, or eye discomfort. These exams can catch potential issues early and provide you with the necessary advice or corrective measures. Ensuring that your vision is not being adversely affected by your writing routine is crucial for your overall health and well-being.

Exercises for Writers

- Hand and Wrist Care: Regular hand and wrist exercises are crucial for writers. Simple stretches, finger flexing, and wrist rotations can significantly reduce the risk of repetitive strain injuries like carpal tunnel syndrome, which are common in professions involving extensive typing. These exercises help maintain flexibility, reduce stiffness, and increase blood circulation, ensuring that your hands and wrists remain healthy and functional.

- Back and Neck Health: Strengthening the muscles in your back and neck is equally important. Exercises like shoulder shrugs, gentle neck tilts, and back stretches can alleviate the tension that often builds up from prolonged sitting and poor posture. These exercises not only provide immediate relief but also contribute to long-term muscle strength and flexibility, helping to prevent chronic pain and discomfort. Remember, we're in this for the long haul.

- Cardiovascular Activities: Incorporating cardiovascular exercises into your routine has numerous benefits for both physical and mental health. Activities like walking, jogging, swimming, or cycling improve heart health, boost energy levels, and enhance mood. Regular cardiovascular exercise also promotes better sleep, increases stamina, and can improve cognitive function, all of which are beneficial for a writer's overall productivity and creativity. Remember, the fact that we chose a profession where we're mostly seated, we're cutting our life short by at least five years. Regularly getting your heart rate up will fight that.

Mindfulness and Relaxation

- Meditation and Deep Breathing: Incorporating meditation or deep breathing exercises into your daily routine can be immensely beneficial in managing stress and maintaining mental clarity. These practices help in calming the mind, improving focus, and reducing feelings of anxiety that can come with the pressures of writing. Even just a few minutes of meditation or mindful breathing each day can have a profound impact on your overall mental state, providing a sense of peace and grounding. I am an incredibly hard worker. It's quite tiring for the people around me. I'll work, then jump up and do the dishes, then back to work, then write down new ideas, off to water the garden and do the laundry, play with my kid, then cycling and stretching, and back to work, for pretty much 15 hours a day (still easier than when my little one was a baby and I was a work-from-home dad; we did that for the first two years, and then she was off to a morning day care). I know I need to have a healthier approach, and I'm getting there. But for now this it what I need to do, and it can sometimes become overwhelming. I know my body and my mind and keep a close eye on my thoughts. I normally just block out bad thoughts, so the moment they start slipping through, I know something's up. Your mind will tell you when it's time to rest, to take a step back, to prevent yourself from those dark pits of depression.

- Cultivating a Balanced Lifestyle: Balancing your writing life with other activities that bring joy and relaxation is essential. Engaging in hobbies, spending time with friends and family, or simply enjoying the outdoors can provide a much-needed respite from the mental demands of writing. These activities not only offer an opportunity to unwind but also help stimulate creativity and provide new perspectives. A balanced lifestyle ensures that writing remains a fulfilling pursuit rather than a source of burnout.

Adopting healthy writing habits is essential for writers. By paying attention to ergonomics, taking regular breaks, caring for your eyes, and staying physically active, you can maintain a healthy, sustainable writing practice. Remember, a healthy writer is a productive writer. Your physical and mental well-being is not just beneficial for you, but it's also reflected in the quality of your writing.

Cultivate genuine connections in the literary community. Offer value and support without expecting anything in return, and watch these relationships flourish.

Chapter 11

The Vital Role of Nutrition in an Author's Life

Remember when I said this book takes a holistic approach to being an author? Well here you go. In the life of an author, where mental agility and creativity are paramount, the importance of a healthy diet cannot be overstated. The right nutrition not only fuels the body but also significantly enhances concentration, sleep quality, mindset, and creative prowess.

Concentration and Cognitive Function: A diet rich in omega-3 fatty acids, found in fish like salmon and sardines, is crucial for brain health. These fatty acids aid in building brain and nerve cells, essential for learning and memory. Whole grains, which release glucose slowly into the bloodstream, keep you mentally alert throughout the day. Nuts and seeds are also excellent sources of antioxidants, Vitamin E, and amino acids, which can help to protect brain health and improve focus. My grandfather always carried a little bag of raisins in his pocket, and he kept farming his little plot of land up until around 92 years of age. I now always keep a Tupperware bowl filled with mixed nuts and dried fruit, because one of my biggest weaknesses is nibbling. At least now I'm sticking to something healthy.

Sleep Quality: Foods that promote good sleep are equally important for authors, as quality sleep is directly linked to cognitive function and creativity.

Almonds and walnuts contain melatonin, a hormone that regulates sleep, and magnesium, which can improve sleep quality. Dairy products, like milk and yogurt, are rich in calcium and help the brain use the tryptophan found in dairy to manufacture sleep-triggering melatonin.

Proper Mindset and Mood: The gut-brain axis plays a critical role in mood and mental health. Fermented foods like yogurt, kefir, and sauerkraut are rich in probiotics, which improve gut health and have been linked to a reduction in stress and anxiety. Leafy greens like spinach and kale are high in folate, which contributes to the production of serotonin, a neurotransmitter that affects mood, happiness, and anxiety.

Creativity: Foods high in antioxidants, such as berries, can combat oxidative stress and inflammation in the brain, potentially fostering creativity. Dark chocolate, in moderation, not only is a mood booster but also increases blood flow to the brain, which can enhance cognitive function and creativity.

A balanced diet, rich in omega-3s, whole grains, antioxidants, and probiotics, plays a significant role in an author's cognitive function, mood, and overall health. By incorporating these foods into their diet, authors can maintain a sharp mind and a creative edge, essential tools in their craft. Remember, what you put in is what you get out.

Chapter 12

Embracing the Long Road of Writing

For aspiring authors, the dream of mastering the craft of writing often sparkles with the allure of instant success and recognition. However, the truth is that writing, like any art form, is a journey—a long, intricate, and deeply personal odyssey that spans years, even decades. Understanding and embracing this journey is crucial for anyone aspiring to make a lasting impact with their words.

The Marathon, Not the Sprint: Writing is a marathon, not a sprint. It's a career that unfolds over time, demanding patience, persistence, and a relentless commitment to growth. Unlike professions where progress can be linear and predictable, writing is an ever-evolving landscape of challenges and learning opportunities. Each story, each character, each sentence penned is a step forward in this marathon.

The Craft of Constant Learning: One of the most beautiful aspects of writing is that it is an endless learning process. Every book you write, every piece of feedback you receive, every revision you make is an opportunity to hone your skills. The literary world is vast, with countless genres, styles, and techniques to explore. The most successful authors are those who remain students of their craft, always eager to learn and adapt. Forgive me for once again highlighting our , where this is exactly what our mission is.

The Resilience in Rejection: Rejection is an integral part of a writer's journey. Even the most celebrated authors have faced their share of dismissals and critiques (I'd bet money that you've already read Stephen King's *On Writing*. Read it, and read it again). The key is to view rejection not as a setback but as a stepping stone. Each 'no' brings with it valuable insights and the chance to come back stronger. Resilience in the face of rejection is what separates those who dream from those who achieve.

The Business of Writing: Writing is not just an art. It's also a business. Understanding the market, building a brand, engaging with readers, and navigating the publishing world are all critical skills for a successful writing career. This business aspect requires as much dedication and skill as the creative process. Just staying up to date with new platforms, tech, apps, plugins for authors, etc. is already a massive undertaking. That's one more example of where a community of authors can help.

The Community of Writers: No writer is an island. The writing community is a rich tapestry of mentors, peers, and readers. Engaging with this community can provide support, inspiration, and opportunities for collaboration. Writing groups, workshops, and literary events are invaluable resources for growth and connection.

The Personal Evolution: As you journey through your writing career, you'll find that it's not just your skills that evolve, but you as a person. Writing challenges you to explore new perspectives, confront your fears, and delve into the depths of human emotion. It's a path of personal growth, as much as professional. Like a fine wine, you'll improve with age and life experience. If every person on earth would read and write more, we'd all be better off.

The Joy of Creation: Amidst the challenges and the long road to mastery, it's crucial to remember the joy of creation. The thrill of bringing characters to life, of weaving narratives, of touching readers' hearts—these are the rewards that make the journey worthwhile.

Becoming a masterful author is a lifelong endeavor. It's a path filled with learning, resilience, business acumen, community engagement, personal growth, and above all, a deep love for the craft of writing. For those embarking on this journey, embrace each step with patience and passion. Remember, the world of writing is not just about reaching a destination—it's about savoring the journey and growing with every word you write.

> The greatest journeys in life all start with one step, or a single word.

Chapter 13

Earning an Extra Income as an Author

For authors, the journey to completing a novel can be a long and arduous one, often requiring a significant investment of time and energy. However, in the midst of this major project, there are creative and practical ways to supplement your income. Think of these as your writing side-hustles—opportunities to keep your creative juices flowing while also adding a little extra to your bank account.

1. Crafting and Selling Short Stories: Short stories are a fantastic way to keep writing and earning while working on a larger novel. They require less time commitment compared to a novel and can be a great outlet for exploring different genres or experimenting with new writing styles. You can sell these stories to magazines, online platforms, or compile them into a collection for self-publishing. This not only brings in some income but also helps build your presence and following in the writing community.

"I've always thought that the horror genre is one in which short fiction works extremely well—the "short, sharp shock." I love reading and writing short stories, but I also love editing anthologies of short stories. While I don't believe that all writers are automatically great editors (or vice versa), I do think it's possible to be good at both. If you've thought about moving into anthology editing, you do need a few particular skills: are you well read in the genre? How's your knowledge of grammar and punctuation? And perhaps most importantly: are you good at working with other writers? If you can answer "yes" to all three of those and you want to edit an anthology, then you should give it a try! After all, there's always more room for great short stories in horror."—**Lisa Morton, presenter of the anthology course on Heartbeat.**

2. Pitching and Editing an Anthology: If you enjoy collaborative projects, consider pitching and editing an anthology. This involves bringing together a collection of stories, often around a particular theme, from various writers. As an editor, you can engage with a wide array of authors, hone your editing skills, and create a unique compilation that appeals to a specific audience. Anthologies can be sold just like any other book, providing a shared platform for all contributors and a new revenue stream for you. Don't always aim for the highest-tier authors right from the start. Begin with a lower-budget anthology. It might not become a best-seller, but it can be financially lucrative for you and the publisher who accepts it.

3. Freelance Writing and Ghostwriting: Freelance writing or ghostwriting can be a lucrative side-hustle and learning experience. This could involve writing articles, blog posts, or even ghostwriting books for others. While this might steer you a bit away from your personal writing style or preferred genres, it offers a steady income and helps sharpen your writing skills.

4. Offering Writing Workshops or Courses: If you have a knack for teaching and sharing knowledge, consider conducting writing workshops or courses. This could be done locally or online, focusing on various aspects of writing, from character development to plot structuring. Not only does this bring in revenue, but it also establishes you as an expert in your field. If you are interested in doing this, be sure to reach out to me on our with a pitch.

5. Patreon or Crowdfunding for Exclusive Content: Platforms like Patreon allow you to offer exclusive content to your audience for a subscription fee. This could be chapters of your novel-in-progress, exclusive short stories, or insights into your writing process. It's a way to build a community around your work and offer something special to your most dedicated fans. I've overseen crowdfunding projects for projects, books, and even just raising a bit of money for our press in general (back when we were still pretty small). Some of our anthology fundraisers have broken Kickstarter records, raising over $50k. Crystal Lake also has a , which I personally oversee. We even have two tiers specifically catered for authors. Be sure to check them out. During Crystal Lake's early years, there were months where we would've really struggled if it weren't for our Patreon page.

6. Write non-fiction: Delving into non-fiction writing can be a game-changer. Non-fiction books tend to have a wider market and are often easier to sell than fiction. They can also lead to lucrative upselling opportunities, such as related courses or workshops. Writing about topics you're knowledgeable in, whether it's a guide on the craft of writing or a deep-dive into a specific genre, can attract readers who are eager to learn and willing to pay for expert knowledge.

Several years ago, I was facing a financial challenge where I had to pay a lump sum to get out of a contract I no longer wanted to be a part of. I leveraged my industry contacts and proposed a non-fiction writing anthology to a fellow publisher. Instead of competing with my fellow publishers, I almost made sure to build and maintain relationships. After a lot of hard work in only a few months, *The Horror Writer* was published through HellBound Books. The book's success resolved my financial issue, enhanced my professional connections, and provided valuable assistance to numerous authors. As a bonus, the book helped establish me as a non-fiction editor. Plus, it's still bringing in money.

> *"I often hear authors complain about a lack of markets or not being able to break into a certain market, and when I suggest they try non-fiction they tell me they don't know how to write it. Here's my response: Write non-fiction just as you would fiction! A great non-fiction piece includes a beginning, a middle, and an end; it should offer memorable characters, a compelling narrative, and polished writing. It absolutely should involve the reader emotionally and leave them satisfied at the end. Writing non-fiction pieces can be a good way for a writer to expand their readership and add to their income, and should be fun to write!"*—**Lisa Morton**

7. Audio Storytelling or Podcasts: The growing popularity of podcasts and audio storytelling opens another avenue for authors. Creating a podcast, either by narrating your stories or discussing various aspects of writing, can attract a different audience and be monetized through sponsorships or premium content offerings. You can easily connect a podcast to your Patreon page.

8. Learn and profit from new skills: Expanding your skillset can open up rewarding side hustles for any author looking to supplement their income. Consider delving into areas like book layout design, cover creation, or producing captivating book trailers (is a great place to start). These skills not only offer a creative outlet but can also be financially beneficial. As you learn to craft visually appealing book interiors or design striking covers, you'll find opportunities to assist fellow authors, enhancing their works' marketability and your own professional network. Creating book trailers is another avenue where storytelling meets digital media, offering a unique way to engage with the literary community. These ventures not only bolster your income but also deepen your involvement in the world of publishing, making you a more versatile and connected writer. As a publisher, I sit up and notice when authors not only present a book to me, but skills they can use to broaden the reach of their books and possibly even save us a bit of money (money that can now be used for other marketing avenues).

While the goal of finishing your novel remains paramount, exploring these side hustles can not only provide additional income but also enrich your skills as a writer. From selling short stories to engaging in collaborative projects like anthologies, or even venturing into teaching and podcasting, each of these avenues offers unique opportunities to expand your horizons and sustain your writing career. Embrace these diverse options, and find the balance that works best for you as you journey through the world of writing.

Chapter 14

Your Greatest Strength
by Scott Nicholson

Secure writers are, by nature, oxymoronic.

Maybe we're more moronic than oxy, but for the moment, let's breathe together.

We must possess incredible egos to believe seven and a half billion people care what we think, much less that those faceless hordes are willing to pay hard-earned money for the privilege. Once we accept the fact that less than a tenth of our potential audience knows English, we enter a comfort zone—we only have to appeal to 500 million people or so!

At the same time, we must be incredibly insecure. We must second-guess every word choice, every use of pretty adjectives, and every stroke of the slavishly delicious whip of adverb avoidance. We have to look at our work with not only the clichéd "jaundiced eye" (cut every damned cliché from your own writing and we won't have these asides anymore), but from the eye of that most valued person, the reader.

As vain as we are, writers do not create stories. We only provide the framework, plant the suggestion, build the bare bones. Readers bring themselves to our words, and that means they meet us halfway. If we have paid attention to our own existence and feelings, then readers can recognize themselves, and together the writer and reader build a mutual experience in which the sum is greater than the parts. Writer plus reader equals story.

So the first step in surrendering the authorial ego is to recognize you are not in control of the story. You won't be able to sit beside the reader and say, "Hey, this is the part where you're supposed to feel sad and hopeless." Or, "Here's where the protagonist overcomes her weakness and finally kicks ass." Maybe if you're reading live at a convention, you can manipulate your audience with theatrics, but when it's a reader and a pillow and your words, it's nothing but words. So make those words come from the deepest well of your heart, the places where you love and live and hurt and scream and pout and dream and die and get reborn.

I get asked to lead a lot of writer workshops, mostly because I don't think very highly of writers. After Shakespeare and Dickens and William Goldman, everybody else has a lot of room for improvement. But that's the basic joy of writing. We know we'll never be perfect, and it's a stretch whether we will ever be decent. At least at our half of the equation. As Orson Scott Card points out, it's never the reader's fault if something doesn't make sense. It's the writer's shortcoming.

At the workshops I teach, I make a point of asking every participant about his or her current project. I don't care whether it's a family memoir, a celebrity biography of someone the writer saw on TV, or a commercial mystery that involves the Vatican and art and some kind of secret society. The plain truth is you have to tell the truth.

And that's where you shine as a writer.

You know the truth.

Don't obey the common bit of wisdom doled out in universities that tell you to "Write what you know." Let's face it, you don't know much, if you consider the physics involved in sending a satellite to Mars, the DNA of a salamander, or the thousands of masters theses written trying to debunk the alcoholism of

William Faulkner. Writers don't know nothing, and only the worst of us think we know a little bit.

So research.

Get the facts when you need them for your story. Google it. Ask people. Plug in the facts and then forget them.

Because only a tiny handful of our audience will ever check up on the details. The overwhelming majority want to know what the story tells them about themselves, what it teaches them about being alive, what it means to have feelings.

At every workshop, I make a point of saying I would never want to trade places with Stephen King, not in a million years and not for a hundred of his multimillion-dollar film deals. Jaws drop. Occasionally, someone will point out that King outsells me by a factor of thousands. I smile then and, for a rare moment in my life when I'm not writing fiction, I'll be honest.

"Stephen King doesn't know my stories," I'll say, pretending I know what I'm talking about while avoiding the pretension that plagues any writing instructor. "He knows his stories, but he's never lived my life. And he's never lived yours. He doesn't know your secrets, but you do. You know where you hurt and where you love. That's your secret weapon. That's your greatest strength. Use it."

Writing what you know doesn't mean you write a banking industry novel if you work as a teller, or a literary novel about impotency if you're a college literature professor. It means telling the emotional truth. You know the truth, even when you deceive yourself about it. The best liars are well aware of their talent. So use it.

Lie to us, and make us believe it. That's the secret of both love and writing. Fool us all, because your greatest strength is what pumps through your heart. Tell it like it is, because you know better than anyone. Don't spare us the pain of your emotional mistakes.

You can only give half the story, and must seduce your reader into the other half. That's why you develop skills. Once you master basic grammar and punctuation, then it's just you and your heart and the truth.

And the reader.

So forget publishers, contracts, agents, bestseller lists, writing advice articles, whatever your writing group or your mother told you. You know better than any of them.

You have lived, and you have earned your truth. You have earned your voice. Get inside yourself, then get over it.

Be an honest liar.

That's the ultimate oxymoron, and the one we'll fall in love with.

Scott Nicholson is the author of The Home, The Manor, The Harvest, The Red Church, *and* The Farm *(2006), as well as the story collection* Thank You For The Flowers. *He won the grand prize in the international* Writers of the Future *contest in 1999, and advises every new writer to give the contest a try.*

Shed the belief in limited success. In the vast literary universe, there's ample space for every voice, including yours.

Until next time

As a publisher/editor/author in the horror writing industry, I've learned some valuable lessons that I believe are crucial for any writer. Some were hard lessons, some expensive, and some I'm only now starting to see the value in after more than a decade of ignoring them. The path of a writer, especially in the realms of horror, can be fraught with unique challenges. Here are some pieces of advice I've gathered over the years:

The Importance of Contracts: Always use contracts, no matter how small the gig may seem. Whether you're offering a service or receiving one, a contract is your safety net. I've found myself in situations where my work or agreement was challenged. In such cases, letting emotions take over can be detrimental. A lawyer friend once advised me to stay calm and refer directly to the relevant clause in the contract. This approach keeps the interaction professional and prevents any miscommunication that could be amplified on social media or other public forums. It's better to have a contract and not need it than to not have it and desperately need it.

Embrace Professionalism as a Public Figure in the Horror Writing Industry: In the horror writing industry, being an author also means stepping into the spotlight and embracing the role of a public figure. Once your work is published, you represent not just yourself but your genre and its community. This visibility demands a professional demeanor, both in person and online.

Your interactions, from book signings to social media posts, shape your public image and professional identity.

Facing public scrutiny is an inherent part of being an author. Criticism and judgment come with the territory, but how you respond to them is crucial. Handling critiques with grace and professionalism, avoiding public disputes, and maintaining a composed online presence are key to building a positive reputation. The best advice is to not even comment on reviews. Bad reviews come with the territory, and if only one or two people nag about something, ignore it. If a few reviewers point something out, then truly consider what they're saying and try to learn from it.

Professionalism also involves striking a balance between engaging with your audience and maintaining personal boundaries. Be thoughtful about what personal information you share, keeping a clear line between your public and private life.

As horror writers, we are more than storytellers. We are influencers and inspirers in our field. Upholding professionalism in every aspect of our public persona is essential. It influences how we're perceived and contributes to our credibility and respect in the industry. Embracing this dual role of author and public figure with commitment and passion is crucial for a successful and respected career in horror writing. Remember, it only takes one bad action to destroy everything you've built up over the years.

Protect Your Emotional and Mental Health: Writing, particularly horror, can take a toll on your mental health. It's essential to maintain a balance. Make sure you're taking care of your emotional well-being. This could mean different things for different people—therapy, meditation, or simply having someone to talk to. Don't let the isolation of writing consume you.

The Necessity of Physical Health and Exercise: Physical health is just as crucial. Regular exercise is not only beneficial for your body but also for your mind. It can be a powerful tool for clearing your head, managing stress, and boosting creativity. Remember, a healthy body fosters a healthy mind, which in turn enhances your writing.

Spending Time with Family and Loved Ones: Never underestimate the value of spending time with family and friends. They are your support system, your sounding board, and often, your escape from the world of horror you delve into. Balancing writing time with family time is key to maintaining a healthy perspective on life.

Living a Life Worth Writing About: Finally, and perhaps most importantly, live a life worth writing about. It's easy for writers, especially in the horror genre, to become reclusive, to get lost in the worlds we create. But stepping out, experiencing life, engaging with the world—that's where true inspiration and happiness lies. Travel, try new things, meet new people, and collect experiences. These are the ingredients that make not just a great writer, but a great story.

Navigating the horror writing industry, or any writing industry for that matter, requires more than just talent and passion. It requires mindfulness about the business side of things, attention to your mental and physical health, a commitment to your relationships, and a dedication to living fully. These are the things that will not only protect you and your career but will also enrich your writing in ways you can't imagine.

Now put down this book and go write.

Author Toolbox

Heartbeat

SCAN ME

Publisher Rocket

SCAN ME

Click Funnel

SCAN ME

Pictory.ai

SCAN ME

JOIN OUR
MASTERMIND!

JOIN THE SHADOWS & INK
MASTERMIND GROUP FOR A
FULL YEAR...

**YES. I WANT
TO JOIN
THE INNER
CIRCLE:**

THE END?

Not if you want to dive into more of Crystal Lake Publishing's Tales from the Darkest Depths!

Check out our amazing website and online store or download our latest catalog here.
https://geni.us/CLPCatalog

Looking for award-winning Dark Fiction?
Download our latest catalog.

Includes our anthologies, novels, novellas, collections, poetry, non-fiction, and specialty projects.

Where Stories Come Alive!

We always have great new projects and content on the website to dive into, as well as a newsletter, behind the scenes options, social media platforms, our own dark fiction shared-world series and our very own webstore. Our webstore even has categories specifically for KU books, non-fiction, anthologies, and of course more novels and novellas.

About the author

Joe Mynhardt stands as a paragon in the horror literary world, a Bram Stoker Award-winning South African publisher, editor, and mentor with over a decade of experience. As the founder and CEO of Crystal Lake Entertainment, Joe has transformed a humble 2012 startup into a multifaceted Intellectual Property powerhouse. Under his visionary leadership, Crystal Lake Publishing has become just one of the many thriving divisions of his company.

With a track record of working with and publishing works by luminaries such as Neil Gaiman, Clive Barker, Stephen King, Charlaine Harris, Ramsey Campbell, John Connolly, Jack Ketchum, Jonathan Maberry, Christopher Golden, Graham Masterton, Damien Angelica Walters, Adam Nevill, Lisa Morton, Elizabeth Massie, Joe R. Lansdale, Edward Lee, Paul Tremblay, and Wes Craven, Joe is the quintessential mentor for aspiring horror authors. His deep industry insights and extensive network place him in a unique position to guide both new and seasoned writers in the genre.

Joe's commitment to nurturing talent and fostering author careers is at the heart of Crystal Lake Entertainment's ethos. His approach is not just about publishing books; it's about building a community, sharing knowledge, and being a beacon of friendship and guidance in the often-intimidating world of horror writing.

Since leaving his day job in 2016 to focus full-time on his passion, Joe has also excelled as a work-from-home dad, a role he embraced in 2018. His daughter, Cayleigh, named after his childhood influences Bruce Lee and Stan Lee, is a testament to his belief in the power of storytelling across all mediums. Joe's love for great narratives extends beyond literature, encompassing comics, games, film, and television, with favorites ranging from Poe, Doyle, and Lovecraft to King, Connolly, and Gaiman.

Joe Mynhardt isn't just a figure in the horror industry—he's a driving force behind it, leading a successful online business that goes beyond the traditional boundaries of publishing. Discover more about Joe's journey and Crystal Lake's offerings at www.crystallakepub.com or connect with him on Facebook or Patreon (includes author tiers and a 7-day free trial), where he continues to inspire and lead the next generation of horror storytellers.

Readers...

Thank you for reading *Shadows & Ink Vol.1*. We hope you enjoyed this on writing guide.

If you have a moment, please review *Shadows & Ink Vol.1* at the store where you bought it.

Help other readers by telling them why you enjoyed this book. No need to write an in-depth discussion. Even a single sentence will be greatly appreciated. Reviews go a long way to helping a book sell, and is great for an author's career. It'll also help us to continue publishing quality books.

Thank you again for taking the time to journey with Crystal Lake Publishing.

You will find links to all our social media platforms on our Linktree page.
https://linktr.ee/CrystalLakePublishing

Follow us on Amazon:

MISSION STATEMENT

Since its founding in August 2012, Crystal Lake has quickly become one of the world's leading publishers of Dark Fiction and Horror books. In 2023, Crystal Lake officially transitioned into an entertainment company, joining several other divisions, genres, and imprints, including Torrid Waters, Crystal Lake Comics, Crystal Lake Games, Crystal Lake Kids, and many more.

While we strive to present only the highest quality fiction and entertainment, we also endeavour to support authors along their writing journey. We offer our time and experience in non-fiction projects, as well as author mentoring and services, at competitive prices.

With several Bram Stoker Award wins and many other wins and nominations (including the HWA's Specialty Press Award), Crystal Lake Publishing puts integrity, honor, and respect at the forefront of our publishing operations.

We strive for each book and outreach program we spearhead to not only entertain and touch or comment on issues that affect our readers, but also to strengthen and support the Dark Fiction field and its authors.

Not only do we find and publish authors we believe are destined for greatness, but we strive to work with men and women who endeavour to be decent human beings who care more for others than themselves, while still being hard working, driven, and passionate artists and storytellers.

Crystal Lake Publishing is and will always be a beacon of what passion and dedication, combined with overwhelming teamwork and respect, can accomplish. We endeavour to know each and every one of our readers, while building personal relationships with our authors, reviewers, bloggers, podcasters, bookstores, and libraries.

We will be as trustworthy, forthright, and transparent as any business can be, while also keeping most of the headaches away from our authors, since it's our job to solve the problems so they can stay in a creative mind. Which of course also means paying our authors.

We do not just publish books, we present to you worlds within your world, doors within your mind, from talented authors who sacrifice so much for a moment of your time.

There are some amazing small presses out there, and through collaboration and open forums we will continue to support other presses in the goal of helping authors and showing the world what quality small presses are capable of accomplishing. No one wins when a small press goes down, so we will always be there to support hardworking, legitimate presses and their authors. We don't see Crystal Lake as the best press out there, but we will always strive to be the best, strive to be the most interactive and grateful, and even blessed press around. No matter what happens over time, we will also take our mission very seriously while appreciating where we are and enjoying the journey.

What do we offer our authors that they can't do for themselves through self-publishing?

We are big supporters of self-publishing (especially hybrid publishing), if done with care, patience, and planning. However, not every author has the time or inclination to do market research, advertise, and set up book launch strategies. Although a lot of authors are successful in doing it all, strong small presses will always be there for the authors who just want to do what they do best: write.

What we offer is experience, industry knowledge, contacts and trust built up over years. And due to our strong brand and trusting fanbase, every Crystal Lake Publishing book comes with weight of respect. In time our fans begin to trust our judgment and will try a new author purely based on our support of said author.

With each launch we strive to fine-tune our approach, learn from our mistakes, and increase our reach. We continue to assure our authors that we're here for them and that we'll carry the weight of the launch and dealing with third parties while they focus on their strengths—be it writing, interviews, blogs, signings, etc.

We also offer several mentoring packages to authors that include knowledge and skills they can use in both traditional and self-publishing endeavours.

We look forward to launching many new careers.

This is what we believe in. What we stand for. This will be our legacy.

Welcome to Crystal Lake Publishing—Where Stories Come Alive!

www.ingramcontent.com/pod-product-compliance
Lightning Source LLC
Chambersburg PA
CBHW070056030426
42335CB00016B/1907